DA/m/
1099

Spanish
Civil War –

FROM SPANISH TRENCHES

from Spanish Trenches

RECENT LETTERS FROM SPAIN

COLLECTED AND EDITED BY MARCEL ACIER

MODERN AGE BOOKS, INC., NEW YORK

*To all those who have toiled and shed
their blood through the ages in order to
live decently by the fruit of their labor*

ACKNOWLEDGMENTS

I wish to thank all those who have given their time and their coöperation to the making of this book. Without their help I could not possibly have collected this material at a time when Spain's fields are still drenched with the blood of its people.

Special acknowledgment is due the following:

The *Chicago Tribune* for permission to reproduce in part the Badajoz article written by Jay Allen, which appeared in the *Chicago Tribune* of August 30, 1936.

The *New York Times* for permission to reprint the Madrid dispatch of Herbert L. Matthews which appeared in the *New York Times* of April 23, 1936.

The New Masses for permission to reprint Pablo de la Torriente Brau's letter from the issue of January 26, 1937; also the article by James Hawthorne which appeared in the issue of June 8, 1937; and the articles by Ilya Erenburg, which are printed for the first time in the United States in this volume.

M. A.

CONTENTS

FOREWORD

Today almost every nation on the earth's surface is represented in Loyalist Spain. The trenches of its war-torn front have seen men and women from the United States, France, and England; freedom-loving exiles from Germany and Italy. Some of these friends of the Spanish people have come from Austria, Switzerland, and Holland; others from the Scandinavian countries, from Poland, from Czecho-slovakia. Yes, even the Far East has contributed to the forces fighting in the International Brigade, or to the rearguard tending the wounded and filling the hundred-and-one jobs that must be disposed of even in time of war.

It is impossible to attempt to represent in this volume all the nationalities that make up the International Brigade. Many letters from men and women born in Italy, in France, and in other countries are not included here though they are at least as important and as interesting as the ones that follow. The editor did not wish to shorten any of the present letters to make room for additions to this collection.

Such additional letters would have to find place in another volume. It would even be possible to collect volumes of letters written by Spaniards themselves — letters from the militiamen at the front, from the men and women whose children and homes have for the past year been prey to fascist terror.

The purpose of this volume is to present the cause of the Spanish people as it is seen through the eyes of those who have gone to their support. To most of them Spain is a strange country, with strange customs and a strange tongue. Only a short time ago they left their homes, their relatives and friends, and their jobs. Their impressions of Spain are fresh and vivid; they see Spain as you would see it yourself — Spain where, in the twelve months which have just passed, almost five hundred thousand human beings — men, women and children of all ages — who had asked only for the right to live free, were instead given death.

Here are letters which tell a story — sincere and from the heart — written to someone back home and not, for the most part, for publication. For this reason no attempt has been made to choose the material for its literary merit. On the contrary, the original style of the writer has been preserved at all times, mistakes have not been corrected; the letters stand as they were written at the front, in the trenches and dugouts, and in the shelled cities and villages of Spain. Some of these letters were written by authors who are masters of their craft, but others were in the labored handwriting of people who seldom have occasion to commit their thoughts to paper. A few of the inclusions were not written as letters. Yet they form a part of this volume because of the emotional stress and obvious sincerity which inspired them. They serve to round out the picture presented by the letters.

There have been two contending social forces in Spain for many years. One of these strove to give the people a constitution and the right to live as free human beings. The other wished to continue its rule over the people of Spain with a fist of iron. These two forces will be discussed in detail in a final chapter. It can only be emphasized here that the constitution won the undeniable victory at the polls over those who would rather burn Spain than relinquish the power they once held.

Marcel Acier

New York City, July 18, 1937

FROM SPANISH TRENCHES

BLOOD FLOWS IN BADAJOZ

JAY ALLEN, who wrote the following dispatch after a visit to Badajoz, was foreign correspondent in Spain for the Chicago Tribune Press Service.

Elvas, Portugal, August 25, 1936

This is the most painful story it has ever been my lot to handle: I write it at four o'clock in the morning, sick at heart and in body, in the stinking patio of the Pension Central, in one of the tortuous white streets of this steep fortress town. I could never find the Pension Central again, and I shall never want to.

I have come from Badajoz, several miles away in Spain. I have been up on the roof to look back. There was a fire. They are burning bodies. Four thousand men and women have died at Badajoz since General Francisco Franco's Rebel Foreign Legionnaires and Moors climbed over the bodies of their own dead through its many times blood-drenched walls.

I tried to sleep. But you can't sleep on a soiled lumpy bed in a room at the temperature of a Turkish bath, with mosquitoes and bed bugs tormenting you, and with memories of what you have seen tormenting you, with the smell of blood in your very hair, and with a woman sobbing in the room next door.

"What's wrong?" I asked the sleeping yokel who prowls around the place at night as a guard.

"She's Spanish. She came thinking her husband had escaped from Badajoz."

"Well, didn't he?"

"Yes," he said, and he looked at me, not sure whether to go on. "Yes, and they sent him back. He was shot this morning."

"But who sent him back?"

I knew, but asked nevertheless.

"Our international police."

I have seen shame and indignation in human eyes before, but not like this. And suddenly this sleepy, sweaty being, whose very presence had been an added misery, took on the dignity and nobility that a fine dog has and human beings most often have not.

3

From Spanish Trenches

I gave it up. I came down into the filthy patio, with its chickens, rabbits, and pigs, to write this and get it over with.

To begin at the beginning, I had heard dark rumors in Lisbon. Everybody there spies on everybody else. When I left my hotel at 4:00 P.M. August 23, I said I was going to Estoril to try my luck at roulette. Several people noted that down, and I hope they enjoyed their evening at Estoril.

I went to the Plaza de Rocio instead. I took the first taxi. I drove around and around and finally picked up a Portuguese friend who knows his business.

We went to the ferry that crosses the Tagus. Once on the other side we told the chauffeur, "Elvas." He looked mildly surprised. Elvas was 250 kilometers (about 150 miles) away. We streaked through an engaging country of sandy hills, cork oaks, peasants with side-burns, and women with little bowler hats. It was 8:30 o'clock when we pulled up the hill into Elvas, "the lock nobody ever opened." But Elvas knows humiliation now.

It had been nine days since Badajoz fell on August 14th. The Rebel armies had gone on — to a nasty defeat at Medellin, if my information was correct, as it sometimes is — and newspapermen, hand-fed and closely watched, had gone on in their wake.

Nine days is a long time in newspaper work; Badajoz is practically ancient history, but Badajoz is one of those damned spots the truth about which will not be out so soon. And so I did not mind being nine days late, if my newspaper didn't.

I know Badajoz. I had been there four times in the last year to do research on a book I am working on and to try to study the operations of the agrarian reform that might have saved the Spanish Republic — a republic that, whatever it is, gave Spain schools and hope, neither of which it had known for centuries.

We began to hear the truth before we were out of the car. Two Portuguese drummers standing at the door of the hotel knew my friend. Portugal, as usual, is on the eve of a revolution. The people seemed to know who "the others" are. That is why I took my friend along.

They whispered. This was the upshot — thousands of Republican, Socialist, and Communist militiamen and militiawomen were butchered after the fall of Badajoz for the crime of defending their

4

Republic against the onslaught of the Generals and the landowners.

Between fifty and one hundred have been shot every day since. The Moors and Foreign Legionnaires are looting. But blackest of all: The Portuguese "International Police," in defiance of international usage, are turning back scores and hundreds of Republican refugees to certain death by Rebel firing squads.

This very day (August 23) a car flying the red and yellow banner of the Rebels arrived here. In it were three Phalanxists (Fascists). They were accompanied by a Portuguese lieutenant. They tore through the narrow streets to the hospital where Señor Granado, Republican Civil Governor of Badajoz, was lying. Señor Granado, with his military commander, Col. Puigdengola, ran out on the Loyalist militia two days before the fall of Badajoz.

The Fascists ran up the stairs, strode down a corridor with guns drawn, and into the governor's room. The governor was out of his mind with the horror of the thing. The director of the hospital, Dr. Pabgeno, threw himself over his helpless patient and howled for help. So he saved a life.

We drove to Campo Maior, which is only seven kilometers (about four miles) from Badajoz on the Portuguese side. A talkative frontier policeman said: "Of course, we are handing them back. They are dangerous for us. We can't have Reds in Portugal at such a moment."

"What about the right of asylum?"

"Oh," he said, "Badajoz asks extradition."

"There is no such thing as extradition for a political offense."

"It's being done all up and down the frontier on orders of Lisbon," he said belligerently.

We cleared out. We drove back to Elvas. I met friends who are as much Portuguese and vice versa.

"Do you want to go to Badajoz?" they asked.

"No," I said, "because the Portuguese say their frontier is closed and I would be hung up."

But they offered to take me through and back again without complications. So we started. Suddenly we drove out of the lane on to a bridge that leads across the Guadiana River into the town of Badajoz. Now we were in Spain. My friends were known. The extra person in the car (myself) passed unnoticed. We were not stopped.

From Spanish Trenches

We drove straight to the Plaza. Here yesterday there was a ceremonial, symbolical shooting. Seven leading Republicans of the Popular Front (Loyalists), shot with a band and everything before three thousand people. To prove that Rebel generals didn't shoot only workers and peasants. There is no favoritism to be shown between the Popular Fronters.

Every other shop seemed to have been wrecked. The conquerors looted as they went. All this week in Badajoz, Portuguese have been buying watches and jewelry for practically nothing. Most shops belong to the Rightists. It is the war tax they pay for salvation, a Rebel officer told me grimly. We passed a big dry goods shop that seems to have been through an earthquake. "La Campaña," my friends said. "It belonged to Don Mariano, a leading Azañista (follower of Manuel Azaña, President of Spain). It was sacked yesterday after Mariano was shot."

We drove by the office of the Agrarian Reform, where in June I saw the Chief Engineer, Jorge Montojo, distributing land, incurring naturally the hatred of the landowners and, because he was a technician following strictly bourgeois canons of law, the enmity of the Socialists, too. He had taken arms in defense of the Republic, and so —

Suddenly we saw two Phalanxists halt a strapping fellow in a workman's blouse and hold him while a third pulled back his shirt, baring his right shoulder. The black and blue marks of a rifle butt could be seen. Even after a week they showed. The report was unfavorable. To the bull ring with him.

We drove out along the walls to the ring in question. Its sandstone walls looked over the fertile valley of Guadiana. It is a fine ring of white plaster and red brick. I saw Juan Belmonte (bullfight idol) here once on the eve of the fight, on a night like this, when he came down to watch the bulls brought in. This night the fodder for tomorrow's show was being brought in, too. Files of men, arms in the air.

They were young, mostly peasants in blue blouses, mechanics in jumpers. "The Reds." They are still being rounded up. At four o'clock in the morning they are turned out into the ring through the gate by which the initial parade of the bullfight enters. There machine guns await them.

Blood Flows in Badajoz

After the first night the blood was supposed to be palm deep on the far side of the lane. I don't doubt it. Eighteen hundred men — there were women, too — were mowed down there in some twelve hours. There is more blood than you would think in eighteen hundred bodies.

In a bullfight when the beast or some unlucky horse bleeds copiously, "wise monkeys" come along and scatter fresh sand. Yet on hot afternoons you smell blood. It is all very invigorating. It was a hot night. There was a smell. I can't describe it and won't describe it. The "wise monkeys" will have a lot of work to do to make this ring presentable for a ceremonial slaughter bullfight. As for me, no more bullfights — ever.

We passed a corner.

"Until yesterday there was a pool blackened with blood here," said my friends. "All the loyal military were shot here and their bodies left for days as an example."

They were told to come out, so they rushed out of the house to greet the conquerors and were shot down and their houses looted. The Moors played no favorites.

Back at the Plaza. During the executions here Mario Pires went off his head. [Mario Pires is a Portuguese newspaper correspondent who had been entirely favorable to the Franco rebellion before his visit to Badajoz.]* He had tried to save a pretty fifteen year old girl caught with a rifle in her hands. The Moor was adamant. Mario saw her shot. Now he is under medical care at Lisbon.

I know there are horrors on the other side aplenty. Almendra Lejo, Rightist, was crucified, drenched with gasoline, and burned alive. I know people who saw charred bodies. I know that. I know hundreds and even thousands of innocent persons died at the hands of revengeful masses. But I know who it was who rose to "save Spain" and so aroused the masses to a defense that is as savage as it is valiant.

"But they didn't burn the jail." I had read in the Lisbon and Seville papers that they had. "No, the brothers Pla prevented it."

I knew Luis and Carlos Pla, rich young men of good family, who had the best garage in southwestern Spain. They were Socialists

*Comments within brackets here and elsewhere are the editor's.

7

because they said the Socialist Party was the only instrument which could break the power of Spain's feudal masters.

They harangued the crowd that wanted to burn the three hundred Rightists in the jail just before the Moors entered, saying they were going to die in defense of our Republic, but they were not assassins. They themselves opened the doors to let these people escape.

"What happened to the Plas?"

"Shot."

"Why?"

No answer.

There is no answer. All these people could have been allowed to escape to Portugal three miles away, but they weren't.

On the moon drenched streets there was a smell of jasmin, but I had another smell in my nostrils. Sweet, too horribly sweet. So back to Elvas.

There in the white Plaza by a fountain, a youth leaning against the wall with his feet crossed was playing his guitar and a soft tenor sang a melting Portuguese love song.

At Badajoz in June boys still sang beneath balconies. It will be a long time before they do again.

Suddenly through the square shot a car with a red and yellow flag. We halted. Our drummers came to meet us.

"They are searching the hotel."

"For whom?"

"Don't know."

We shall go away, as soon as it is light. People who ask questions are not popular near this frontier, if it can be called a frontier.

THE AMERICAN HOSPITAL UNIT

THE AMERICAN HOSPITAL UNIT was organized to relieve the distressed and the suffering in Spain. It serves all wounded alike, regardless of their political faith; civilians as well as soldiers. A number of American base hospitals and ambulances are functioning in Spain today, thanks to the gifts of American people who abhor the atrocities of war.

Those who went over, physicians as well as nurses, are hopelessly overworked; working forty hours without sleep or rest is not unusual for these men and women. Practically all of these people left good positions in the United States to donate their services to those who were wounded and maimed. They volunteered for an indefinite period: as long as there might be need for them in Spain. They can return at any time if they so wish.

DR. EDWARD K. BARSKY is chief surgeon and head of the personnel of the American Hospital Unit in Spain. He left his flourishing practice in the hands of his brother, likewise a physician, to whom this letter is addressed. Dr. Barsky was assisting surgeon on the staff of the Beth Israel Hospital in New York City. He studied medicine at Columbia, and was graduated from its college of Physicians and Surgeons in 1919. Post-graduate courses in surgery took him to Berlin, Vienna and Paris. He has been a member of the New York County Medical Association for a number of years.

Dr. Barsky assisted in the organization of the Medical Bureau to Aid Spanish Democracy before leaving for Spain.

                    Hotel Ingles, Valencia, February 12
                         (Hard to keep track of date)

Dear Arthur:

Just a line to let you know that everything is O.K. Had lots of receptions, etc., and saw many very interesting things. Was in Madrid for a few days — wonderful morale of all the people and especially the soldiers — took a short trip out into the trenches and everything seemed fine. Very good hospital facilities — well or-

9

ganized and no need of us there. Tomorrow will start for Albacete and then start to get started. It's all a very complicated and slow process — but once started, there'll be plenty to do.

Have many things to write about — but so many that it's difficult to start. So far, everything has gone fine — and the few discomforts and disappointments are to be expected, and in truth slight. Sure that matters will turn out well — and when I get back, I'll have plenty of good stories to tell.

In our trip to and from Madrid, we passed through some beautiful country — and so peaceful that it's hard to realize that there is a war. The sleepy quiet little villages — old — still — are terrific contrasts to what one expects — especially with the women walking about and the kids playing around.

Things in Madrid are really remarkable — especially when you realize the terrific time they have been having. Cafés crowded, — people in the streets — and nowhere the amount of destruction the N. Y. papers would lead you to believe. The telephone building still stands.

Hope you're not worrying about me — nothing to worry about. I feel fine — really as well as I ever felt. Tell all the folks that writing comes very hard — Don't find much time to write for some reason — but remember me to all and someday I'll drop them lines.

Take good care of yourself — and write me — but remember, answers will be slow as the mail takes some time.

Love to all — be good.

EDDIE

I know you'll think this a very unsatisfactory letter — but the thing to get is that I feel and am O.K. — and how are you all?

MILDRED RACKLEY joined the Hospital Unit as clerk and interpreter. Her knowledge of a number of languages is of great importance, since most of the Americans spoke no language besides their own. Miss Rackley is a native of Carlsbad, New Mexico. She is of Scotch-Irish extraction; one of her ancestors was John Smith, famous in early American history.

She graduated from the University of Texas and later studied art in Germany, Italy and Spain.

The American Hospital Unit

Precious, darling Bobbie:

We got your letters in Barcelona, and they were terribly comforting. So many things have been happening that our heads are in a whirl.

Since Barcelona, where we met Luis Companys, President of Catalonia, and other officials, and I got our freight across the border, we were convoyed down to Valencia. There we were again besieged by countless official receptions. Eddie [Dr. Barsky] says his is a boring war! Because we haven't done anything yet.

Eddie, Miss Martin and I left Valencia four days ago with a representative of the Health Dept., a chauffeur and a guard with a machine gun in a Rolls Royce, for Madrid, where we made a tour of the front line trenches.

While looking over to the enemy line a couple of hundred yards away, a bullet sang past Eddie's right ear. We both ducked. There was not much shooting that day. We were being conducted by Lieut. Col. Ortega who is the commanding officer in the sector of University City.

We were quartered in the Hotel Florida, which is only three blocks away from the telephone building, which despite newspaper reports, is whole and has only a few cannon holes in the top part. We, E. and I, went over to give Matthews and the other correspondents a story, and everything is functioning normally.

At night in the hotel and in the streets, which are completely unlighted, we could hear the reports of guns and mortars only a mile and less away. It was a peculiar sensation. Everything in the city still and sleeping, an occasional car darting through the dark streets, stars twinkling overhead, and the rumbling of guns not very far away. In the daytime, the streets are absolutely filled with people. There was no air raid while we were there. The morale of the population is superb — invincible, triumphant.

Even though they are rationed — bread, meat, and cigarettes — life goes on as if no war existed. The government is having a hard time trying to evacuate the civil population which is greater in Madrid than usual because suburbs in the fighting areas have moved into the city and a food shortage resulted.

We also visited numbers of hospitals, first aid stations, and

11

classification stations in order to get a perspective of the hospitaliz-
ation in Madrid. They have plenty of hospitals and have even con-
solidated some for efficiency's sake.

On other fronts the need for assistance is much greater, and we
expect to open a hospital on a front where we are needed more
badly.

The officials of Madrid were more than cordial and hospitable to
us. We had dinner one evening in the Ministry of Finance — where
we were the guests of honor, and we met all the generals in the
fighting around Madrid — Ortega — a Basque defending the University City sector, Galan, Fanjul, Sabio, Romero, besides the administrator of the Min. of Health & Finance and the Pres. of the
Spanish Red Cross.

The main road from Madrid to Valencia was threatened by
cannon and tanks, so we had to return by a wretched by-road down
here, where we spent the night and visited a base hospital —
where we are sitting now. This hospital is established in a palace
belonging formerly to one of the wealthy landlords of Spain. It is a
gorgeous place.

We are leaving for Albacete in a few minutes — Tomorrow we
will return to Valencia.

Have to stop — finish later.

Valencia: two days later

Leaving now for Albacete. Eddie spoke of you last night. All love
to you and Joe and the children.

Mildred

Albacete, Spain

Medical Bureau to Aid Spanish Democracy,
381 Fourth Avenue, New York, N. Y.

Dear Friends:

We are now settled in a new school house, with no sanitary facilities (we all wonder how the Spaniards manage), a very feeble electric line, no telephone, no water, and a pretty awful road. We went
immediately to the alcalde (mayor), head of the Popular Front,
asking him for the full cooperation of the village in the installation
and operation of the hospital. They did absolutely everything for

us. We had dozens and dozens of men carrying out school desks and tables, the electricians were wiring the building for lights, the telephone service were installing two telephones, all the masons in the village were working the entire night knocking through a wall to connect the upper and lower floors. Another crew were unloading trucks, still another opening crates, and an army of women were sweeping and washing floors. There was no place to eat, and no kitchen in the building.

We had orders to open the hospital for work in forty-eight hours, and we were giving everything we had, every one of us — to have the hospital ready.

On the third day, the patients began to pour in. We got forty the first day.

The roads for six kilometers on either side of us were so bad that it would have killed a patient to take him over them in ambulances. We spoke to the alcalde, and the next day all the peasants were forbidden to go to the fields, and literally thousands of men — all those not fighting at the front — were working on the road, carrying baskets of stones and filling in the holes, then baskets of earth to put around the stones. I can't tell you the feeling it gave me when we took the first bus over the road, and all along the way, Salud! Salud! from every one of them.

Practically all the soldiers we got were badly wounded, and all had to have operations. Many of them were shot through the skull, others through the chest, and numbers of them had nasty abdominal perforations. Every operation that Dr. Edward Barsky performed was really a work of art. And every member of the staff has helped whenever possible and in every way with all kinds of work. One night at 2 o'clock, in the middle of an operation, the battery went dead. All of us ran for our flashlights, and with the feeble glimmer of eight flashlights, Dr. Barsky finished removing a shattered kidney.

Last week we had about sixty coming in in a few hours, the doctors and nurses were working forty hours without stopping, going from one major operation to the next.

You will see from this the pressing need for able surgeons in all fields. Besides the initial seventeen in our American personnel we have about fifty people working for us, including eight chauffeurs, nine cooks, ten assistant nurses, ten washwomen, scrubwomen, seamstresses, stretcher carriers, etc.

We have to have more surgeons, nurses, ambulances and supplies, and we have confidence in you that you will send them.

Fraternally,

MILDRED RACKLEY

↔

RAY HARRIS is a young nurse who has been associated with the Lebanon Polyclinic and Bellevue Hospital in New York City.

American Hospital No. 1, Soccoro Rojo, Albacete, Spain,
February 27, 1937

Dear Sally —

Here's more of the adventures that befell. . . Landed in Port Bou from Paris, sitting up in the train. Was of course seen off by a delegation, among them John Langdon-Davies, the English writer, "Behind the Spanish Barricades." More about him later. At Port Bou, the Spanish Border — got in 8 A.M. tired and hungry — the scenery on the way down was beyond words or descriptions — snow capped mountains — sparkling sea (Mediterranean) and gay colored grounds and villages. At the port we were met by a very handsome Spanish Captain — whom we all took to and he on the other hand, said he felt very ill and needed nursing — you know the old story. So —, after a lunch of a variety of foods and liquors and of course, a toast with champagne again. (Gee, you should see us drink wine — we demand it now!) After a heavy lunch and no sleep — with the little tavern very crowded — the problem of sleep came up — where was the town going to put up some 17-odd people. We were put up in grand style, though. They opened the railroad station hotel for us — the most modern building in the town — even a bathroom between two rooms (no hot H_2O). Nevertheless, everyone pitched in, making our beds — even the chief commandant.

So to bed and did we sleep. We were wakened at nine o'clock (By the time we got to bed it was three or four — time doesn't seem to matter here. Lunches and dinners take two–three hours —

tell that to Blumey). We had supper and took walks up the mountain paths, all very nice, etc. The next A.M. about eleven — big touring cars came and took us to Barcelona. What cars. Some had insignias — must have been a count's or some big shot, at one time. Then some more swell views and scenery and arrived at Barcelona about eight at night. Nice hotel — I think I sent you some cards from there. We stopped at Hotel Oriente, a good enough place. Stayed for about five days, where things happened. Met J. Langdon-Davies, got his snapshots — took us touring about town (all this time the big cars and chauffeurs were at our disposal so that we saw a good bit of the town). Saw a command performance of a dance festival — finished at two A.M. Folk dances.

Were we tired. What struck me funny: Imagine the officials of New York City taking visitors to the CAMEO. Well, we were. We were taken to see WE ARE FROM KRONSTADT — and had box seats. Are you laughing?

By the way, J. Langdon-Davies threatened to put us in his next book. Met lots of boys on leave in Barcelona — took in dances, walks, etc. People sit in cafes all day — meet, have business, in fact even children are brought in to have coffee (undrinkable), milk, etc. On to Valencia, again in cars. We saw a lot of Spain, speeding through towns. Valencia not as interesting as Port Bou, but nice. Met Dr. Bethune, swell guy very busy. Stopped at a place called Hotel Inglis, where nobody spoke English. This certainly was a seething place — all sorts of reporters — who were forever curious about us — men who came to sell or buy things — we even had a hotel SIREN — probably a chorus girl at one time — waiting for a boy friend or something. Anyway, we went to a CHARITY bull fight! And she was in our party. Were we stared at — she looks like Jean Harlow. The bull fight is not a pleasant thing to watch — none are really fought any more nowadays, though. This one we saw was a fancy dress and comic fight — so we all had a laugh.

About this time I understand telegrams were sent out, about us being in Madrid, which is wrong of course. Our leader and Head Nurse did go out to see about a site for the hospital. We stayed in Valencia three or four days.

Then on to Albacete — a seething military town — where I

guess I can't say too much in a letter. Make note and I'll try to recall facts. We travelled to Albacete in big trucks and our ambulances. The nice, comfortable touring cars were gone from now on. No more grand style. The Americans had made their splash — so what.

We met a Lady Hastings in Barcelona, who was with the English Medical Unit and she told us what a good impression we made. Nice woman. She was ill. We took turns taking care of her.

Then on to our destination — again I'll just mention the name — *El Romeral* — not even on the map. Make another note, especially about travelling down to El Romeral. . . I'll tell you about it. We found a building which just about suited us. Of course no running hot and cold water or toilet or shower. Another note: I'm going to soak next time I reach a bath tub. So we started unpacking and unloading our stuff. We had the whole town about us.

I'm writing this in the kitchen at four A.M. Yet, again I'm on night duty, but this time I don't mind it. We have some Spanish women in to help us. I don't overwork — but we are busy — and do we need trained help. Do you know when the other Unit is coming over? I'm going around the hospital to make the rounds now. We have an upstairs and a downstairs and we have a staff house across the lane. Two nice Englishmen with an ambulance were attached to us and one of our M.D's is trying to play matchmaker. Wow — chilly and clear around here. We're very high above sea level. The days are nice but — oy — the nights are cold. You should hear me jabber away in Spanish, with a vocabulary of about fifteen words, and hands — I just about get along. Just brought in food from our storehouse. I go around with a big batch of keys and give materials to our little Spanish night cook. Maurice is sitting opposite me and buttering bread for the patients' breakfast. By the way, reading matter is important here. The only papers we get is the English Daily, and the latest is February 10th — any sort of reading matter but soon!

Love and regards to everyone, thanks for the note to Grandma —

RAY

The American Hospital Unit

FREDERICKA MARTIN went to Spain as head nurse of the American Hospital Unit. She is a graduate of the nursing school of Christ Hospital in Jersey City, N. J., and was on the staffs of Bellevue, Fordham and Lying-In Hospital of New York City. She left her position as head nurse in another hospital to volunteer for duty in Spain. She sailed with Dr. Barsky in January 1937.

March 20, 1937

Anna dear:

I have heard just twice from the States and one note mentioning the fact that you were busy organizing a Women's Auxiliary to the Medical Bureau. So during this lull I'm going to try to write an appeal for you to transmit to your women associates to see if you can rally some support and aid for my girls.

Will you remember me to your nice Dr. Miller? I always think of him when I flit thru the store room and see the gauze and cotton stacked nearly to the ceiling in one corner and wonder what we'll do when it is gone and if none from the States will reach us. The lovely blanket you contributed is warming such a splendid young Spanish boy right now. We are all cowering in the present rainy damp weather inside these stone walls, even in bed with hot water bottles and we have to pile blankets on our poor patients until they are nearly worn out by the weight alone. I am still clinging to the sweater you gave me. I have never been outside the hospital grounds since the day we arrived here and I see children only in the distance through the windows.

We have been here three weeks this afternoon. We started to unload our furniture about four o'clock. Two days later we received patients and worked madly day and night until a few days ago. Since then we have received only one or two patients a day. I wish I could convey my pride in my girls. They have been superhuman. They have never lost their cheerful spirit or quarreled with each other or grumbled. Not *once* has a nurse been for a stroll. You see it is the nurse that oils the cogs of the hospital machinery. She prepares for the operations while the doctors sit and wait. And all the time she is caring for the patients. And except for one dreadful night when the floors were covered with wounded men on stretchers

17

and borrowed mattresses, the patients here have had as good nursing care as any ward patient in New York City and better than
many. We have thirteen Spanish girls whom we are trying to train
but the results have been pretty hopeless up to now. Most of the
actual work was done by our handful. When I tell you the girls had
such swollen feet that some of them had to wear floppy patients'
slippers in order to walk, it must sound unreal. But it is true.

I wish you would tell Jack Kahn how wonderful Sally has been.
She has charge of our top floor with beds for fifty-four patients and
space for extra mattresses. If you could have seen with your own
eyes how neat and orderly those wards looked, the beds in orderly
lines, the corners of the beds neat and trim, and the faces of the patients, smiling, contented and happy. Our greatest reward is the
grief that the patients display when they have to be moved on to
the larger base hospital. And people come back from the front with
stories that our fame has spread and all the boys want to be sent to
Romeral if they are wounded.

The only trouble with Sally is that I cannot get her off duty at
night. She is supposed to work from seven to seven in the day and
Lini Fuhr has the three wards on the lower floor for the same hours.
At night, Ray Harris works on both floors, with six Spanish girls to
sit around and watch the patients and give them drinks and keep
their hot water bottles filled. But every hour or so after seven I
would spend a futile few minutes with Sally extracting a promise to
go over to bed and then an hour later, I'd find her still on duty.
And she would plead "But Freddie, I just had to do this for this patient. He's suffering so." And I would scold her like the devil and
love her all the more for her devotion. At times there is no question
of any nurse working less than sixteen hours a day or more. But
these scenes took place when we were beginning to slow down a bit a
few days ago. And yesterday Sally did collapse and is ill. All but one
nurse has been ill in bed for two days and the cause was overwork.
You can imagine how eagerly I am looking forward to the addition
of more nurses to our group. I hope the Committee has not forgotten our need in the excitement of preparing a new hospital outfit.
If they cannot send us nurses, they could ship over six brawny
women and assure our keeping on working. For if we get no reinforcements after six months all of us will be ready for the scrap

18

heap. And four or six women, nurses, now, would mean we could manage the work and keep going for years.

I suppose you wonder what the rest of us are doing. I spoke of three nurses. Anna Taft and Helen Freeman work in the operating room — night and day. For there are tremendous technical preparations between periods of continuous operating. When poor Taft stands for ten to twelve hours in her gown and gloves, assisting first one doctor operating and then another and Helen runs back and forth, real perpetual motion at last.

Our lab. technician, Rose Freed, sandwiches in a great deal of nursing along with her laboratory work and is a peach. Myself — I don't know what I do or don't do really. I had to plan meals for the two kitchens, run the cleaning women, laundresses, two dreamy Don Juans who are supposed to be stretcher bearers and are just too elusive for words, always vanishing into thin air, buy some supplies in the village, give the nurses a helping hand everywhere and mother all the personnel. When I cracked up a few days ago, I had a record of three sleepless nights and a maximum four hour nap one night. And the first day I spent in bed I was delirious at times and issuing orders in English and in Spanish for every sort of job. The strain has been terrible for it was just one million times more difficult to do since I had only a few words of Spanish and signs to see that most of the work was done. I didn't crack from the strain but a patient walking from the ambulance fainted and there was only another girl there and we had to get him into the house. And lifting him I strained myself but after two days in bed I'm hale and hearty again. Only once I was down, the nervous strain had a chance to express itself.

Now I could write stories for hours, if I had the hours, and I only wish I could so you could shout them aloud. But I do want to beg you, to show this to Mrs. Feltenstein and others of the Committee and tell them about my girls and tell them I'm crying out for a few more nurses to help my girls before they are worn out.

If you want to help us or know individuals who would like to send supplies to us, here are suggestions, candy, fruitcake, crackers, cheese and fish pastes, cigarettes, of course, George Washington coffee. Small parcels are more apt to reach us than large. Whenever we are working at a headlong tempo, I am still able to fish down into my trunk and bring out a treat. You see on the boat we girls decided to save our boxes of candy for Spain and they were entrusted to me to dispense when I thought them most needed. I can still, as I said, provide another dozen treats, when work is terrific and goat meat or beans seem so difficult to swallow, I put two pieces of candy on a plate and put it in the center of the table and a cry of joy goes around and a yell that "Ma" is on the job again. It's very thrilling and I hope I can keep on contriving odd bits of surprises for them. They deserve so much, but it depends on the old U.S.A. and I am writing begging letters to a few people so that it can be kept up.

I had a small fruitcake and one day we had such a strain and a patient we all loved, died and I made tea and called them into my room and fed each one a tablespoon of fruitcake. We had no knives at the time — hence the tablespoon. The result was dynamic. Anne stopped shivering, Sally's lips got a bit of color in them, etc. And I wished I had brought a trunkful of fruitcake for them.

Two things occurred to me without rereading this scrawl which I am writing so hastily in an effort to utilize a free hour, never knowing when an ambulance will drive up and the mad rush begins again. One is that you may wonder why I write as if we had been here for years when we came here three weeks ago today. Well, a day seems ten weeks, sometimes a year. It seems as if we had been here for months and New York is a faint and unreal dream. All our lives we seem to have been running back and forth along these cold corridors, all our lives we have hated white moonlight because it means the birds of death are busy nearby, sometimes close to us and never did we consider moonlight beautiful or an aid to romance. All our lives we have been hating as we have learned to hate here, when we see the ravages of dum dum bullets in the flesh and bones of the best youth of all the world. The other thing I wanted to mention is the special strain of this nursing. There is nothing impersonal about it. Those patients are our comrades, are a part of us. When they suffer, we suffer and learn to hate them more. There is a terrific emotional drain always. If you have any voice in the committee, beg them to send us more nurses and doctors. Don't let them forget us. They can never fill the need here but they must never stop trying.

My best to you,

FREDDIE

The American Hospital Unit

ROSE FREED was born on New York's East Side in 1911. Her mother was a descendant of Isaac Serveter, famous Rabbi who fled Spain during the Inquisition.

Though born in New York, she spent most of her childhood in Ohio. She became a laboratory technician in the Greenpoint Hospital in 1933 and left that position to go to Spain in the same capacity in January 1937.

The letters are to her brother.

Hotel Oriente, Barcelona, Enero — 31 — 37

Dear Lou,

Left Paris with John Langdon Davies, famous British author, who saw us off to Cerbère. We travelled all afternoon and night, arriving there in the morning. With the Pyrenees on one side and the blue Mediterranean on the other, it was really like entering Paradise. There is no country in the world more beautiful than Spain. It is hard to imagine a heinous war in this idyllic country. We stayed at Cerbère until late afternoon, at which time Spanish soldiers came to escort us into Spain. We entered a large bus and started up the Pyrenees! The roads were perfect. For two hours we travelled up the mountain, and then to Port Bou. Radios installed in the trees shouted greetings to us. With our armed escorts and our uniforms the people were thrilled and cheered us wildly as the word got around as to who we were.

We were escorted to a very beautiful restaurant. My first meal in Spain was an experience in itself! First we were served with anchovies, then octopus and rice! Dr. Barsky told us that we must eat everything we were served or the people would be offended. I think now that Barsky was merely having some malicious joy. I don't think it necessary to describe the extreme uncomfort around the table. Of course they served beef steak too, but I think I shall never understand how octopus ever became Spain's favorite dish. I shudder at the thought that it may be placed before me again.

We went rowing on the Mediterranean later that day. To keep from becoming poetic I won't say anything about that. I'm sure you'll understand.

From Spanish Trenches

We were installed in an ancient castle, whose interior had been renovated during the World War. For the first time in twenty years it was opened — for us! With armed guards to watch over us we spent a restful night. We stayed in Port Bou for two days and then in private cars draped with American and Catalonian flags left for Barcelona, where we are now. We have been in Barcelona for four days now, and on the go from 10 a.m. to 3 a.m. It is impossible to tell you how the Spanish people have catered to us. There is nothing we wish that is not granted to us. They look upon us almost as saviors. I feel embarrassed when I remember that ours is a common cause. What sufferings these poor people must have endured to display such gratefulness towards our puny aid! They cut their choicest flowers and bring them as their humble offerings to our feet. At times I feel moved to tears, and you know how hard boiled I am, don't you. My room is flooded with roses, hyacinths, narcissus, carnations, enormous violets and of course (conilliers!). Never in all my life have I ever seen such beautiful flowers. The roses measure 6″ in diameter.

We were taken to most of the Moorish Ruins and deserted Cathedrals and palaces. I have just come from the Palace of Luis Companys, President of Catalonia, where we were his guests. Movietone pictures were taken of us in the Orange grove garden of the Palace. This palace was built in the thirteenth Century. The beauty of Sert's murals, the gargoyles, the gold inlay ceilings and the huge crystal chandeliers were breathtaking. I left entranced. How bitter the thought that Franco and his Fascist horde is burning, plundering, destroying, yes, raping glorious Spain.

One day five of us girls decided to take a walk. Barcelona under normal conditions has one and a half million people. Now there are thrice that number as refugees continue to pour in from the surrounding countrysides, and the streets are more crowded than Fourteenth St., New York. Some Hungarian Gypsies started to annoy us, even after we had given them several pesetos apiece. An Englishman and several dutch boys came to our rescue — quite timely — and gallantly led us away. The Englishman was — John Langdon Davies! It was as though meeting a long lost friend again. He took us shopping and then to lunch at the Ritz Hotel. This hotel, he said, was the most beautiful hotel in the world (and he should know too!). He had travelled over the world, he said, and had never seen a more glamorous one. On the first floor the orange groves shielded the gambling tables under high brilliant lights, as the rich played and enjoyed their stay in Barcelona — enjoyed the marble floors and stairways and balconies, and magnificent murals. But all that now is like the distant past. When the revolution broke out, the waiters and cooks took over the hotel and made a cooperative restaurant out of it. This restaurant now seats 3,000 people at one sitting. None of its beauty has been marred. Of course some of the furnishings have been moved out in order to seat so many people. The waiters are scrupulously careful that nothing is injured in any way. Davies then took us to an ice cream stand where we had a poor imitation of the American soda. We went back to the Hotel to dress and then attended a musical and ballet given in our honor. Davies, always close to us now, sat in our box. He took us on a tour through Barcelona the next day, God bless him.

The Spanish men, especially the Captains that have been assigned to escort us in these various towns are very fine and gallant. Franco may win the war (may! mind you!) but never will he conquer such determined spirits. It is obvious that he has no popular support.

Well, I must dress to meet La Pasionara tonight. I have been writing this letter in spasms for three days now, and have given up a theatre engagement to finish it, for we are leaving for Valencia Wednesday or Thursday. I'm anxious to get to work. From Valencia we are going to Madrid. The receptions are tiring, but the sight of the almond trees and olive trees in bloom now are never so. I love this velvet grass, these beautiful palms and huge cactus, the semi-tropical climate, this soft, melodious southern air. Although humanity is plentiful the humidity is negligible. Lovely Spain, cool breezes and warm suns — and Franco! A hard to imagine paradox . . .

Have my friends write to me. We would all rather receive letters from home than sleep.

Lots of love to every one.

ROSE

P.S. I don't think I'll learn Spanish, but I may come back speaking broken English.

From Spanish Trenches

Dear Lou:

We left Romeral a little over a week ago. We are in Tarancon now. In another week or so we shall move again. In Romeral we put up in what I thought was a sanitorium, but I read too that it was a school house. It certainly was a modern beautiful building. The efficiency of the hospital was like that of one in peace and not war. When I did not work forty hours at one stretch I was night charge nurse. In fact, that's what I'm doing just now. It is 5:30 A.M., and I've just finished making the rounds of our three hospitals — giving medications and hypos and dressing wounds and circulating in the operating room.

I worked all day and night, then went to Romeral to pick up my laboratory (I do laboratory work too) and back to work again. Driving for seven hours at one hundred and twenty kilometers an hour upset my nervous system a bit.

I was very glad to hear that Dr. B. is doing such good work for Spain. The money you collected could best be used in buying a small generator. We need one badly. A few days ago Tarancon was bombarded. I explained that there are three hospitals here that we are in charge of. Hospital #3 is on the Valencia Road, and that of course was the target. One grape fell about five yards from the hospital, crashing all the windows and breaking the water main. For four days there was no water for the patients.

When a bombardment is expected the lights are put out. If the surgeon happens to be operating they must continue with only the dim rays of the flash light. If we had our generator we could supply our own electricity and would not have to depend upon a central plant.

We need 1,000 more beds, 14,000 more sheets, 3,000 more pillow cases, 7,000 blankets and 2,000 mattresses. A hospital that has 120 beds and all beds occupied may receive 400 more patients in one evening. The boys suffer so much — there is no reason why we cannot have a bed for each one instead of using the floor or a narrow stretcher when they are in excruciating pain.

I need not mention the fact that nurses and surgeons are in great demand. The money raised for Spain should help our plight very much. There is little food here and if possible send us at least 500 pounds of good chocolate bars, as much sugar as possible and as many cigarettes as money can buy.

It is three days now that I started to write this letter. It is March 23 now at twelve noon. We have just evacuated many patients to the base hospitals and the doctors and nurses have collected in my room. I cannot sleep.

Last night it was Dr. Goland's birthday. We made a party at the American Casa. I made rounds and came to see how things were going at the party. We had just given Dr. Goland his birthday present, which consisted of one dozen tooth brushes each in the center of a cup cake with bristles exposed and blue ribbon tied to each, when at twelve midnight the lights went out. We heard the roar of planes. There was a long silence in the room. I spoke. I said I was going to the hospital. Dr. Bloom shouted, "If you think anything of your life don't go." Dr. Barsky said he was going to the hospital. I ran to hospital #3 on the Valencia Road, Dr. Barsky went to hospital #1, and Dr. Odio to Hospital #2. I stayed outside the door of the hospital searching the brilliantly studded starry sky for a sight of the planes, but they were too high and had no lights. They circled overhead many times, they came lower and lower and the sound of the motors became louder and louder. I ran into the hospital only to find some of the Spanish infermos in hysterics. They could not be blamed, they who so many times have been terrorized by the lousy tactics of the fascists, and whose minds reflected the fatalities of such terrorism, and whose fathers, brothers, sweethearts and husbands died on the battlefield singing as their last strength ebbed out for the cause of democracy and love for humanity — could they be blamed for hysteria when they realized what was coming? What right had I to be frightened, I who have just tasted what they have long lived through? With my heart pounding almost as loudly as the roar of the motors above, I spoke to them. I told them they must be brave. I told them that they must comfort their brothers of Spain who are lying in bed helpless, most of them unable to move. I felt strong and stern — what did it matter — our lives to be sacrificed for so many that they may continue to live in peace. They clung to me with an almost deadly grip, kissed me and dried their tears. The crash — you cannot — never can anyone realize the horror of what seems like the earth opening beneath you — the light of the magnesium flare bomb to see if they struck right — and then eight more crashes — then silence, too long, and shrapnel flying in all directions. I ran to Hospital #1, then to Hospital #2, then back to my post where I found all crying silently. I made them all go to sleep and stayed on alone. Later in the morning Dr. Sorrel took the post with me.

You ask me to write of the Spanish people. All I can say is that they are the most simple, most grateful and most lovable people in the world. They are first starting to realize conditions in Spain and the world, but I am isolated from them. I am with the soldiers — how can I write more about them?

I judge the spirit by the soldiers. An ambulance came in with thirty wounded. We started to take care of their wounds and bandage them before we put them into bed. A young Spaniard (he must have been sixteen years old at the most) became impatient. He took out his penknife, cut open the palm of his hand and removed the superficial inflicted bullet (all this without our knowledge). Then he held up his wounded hand in a salute, and holding the penknife in the other with the bloody bullet, shouted: "Comrade medico, salud." And holding his head high he continued and shouted, "No pasaran!" In Spanish "No pasaran" means that Franco shall not pass. The bullet, you see, did not pass through the palm of his hand. It was in but not deeply imbedded. How's that for spirit!

I should love to have newspapers. Also literature. Answer soon and I shall look for time to write more often. Tell them not to worry and that I have received a medal — a star and stripe.

Lots of love to all,

ROSE

April 20, 1937

Dear Lou:

I am in anything but a writing mood. I've yelled at Barsky and snapped at Goland. They think that I'm becoming a psyco. Barsky has become so sweet to me this evening that I'm beginning to feel guilty. He's experienced my temper for the first time. Helen just told me that people are starting to fear me. Well, I guess it's because I haven't been very busy lately.

The American Hospital Unit

I was awakened at 5 o'clock yesterday morning and was asked to go to Valencia for a three day vacation. I refused, and Dr. Barsky was rather surprised. When asked to give my reason for refusing a vacation (an unheard of thing!), I simply said that I preferred Madrid. And so in another day or so I shall leave for Madrid. Madrid is about 2 hours from where we are now.

We have just opened a new base hospital — Villa Paz. Villa Paz was the home of a member of the royal family. It is a beautiful palace with 12 sq. miles of ground. There is a rapid brook with a most picturesque falls. The foliage is dense and looks more like a tropical country than the countryside of Valencia, which is quite tropical. On the outside of every door of the almost innumerable rooms is a small sign which reads that this house was taken over by the Republican Socialists. The owner's maid, who was so very haughty before the revolution, now must carry wood for all of the villagers. I understand that this palace, whose walls are adorned with priceless paintings and tapestries, was actually occupied for only two months during each year — just so the owner could collect taxes from the slaves, who tilled her soil from early dawn to late sundown merely for the compensation of dirty, sunless, cold and damp homes.

These very slaves are today sitting at our table, eating the same food we eat, and eating out of the finest china dishes, upon which the crown and the coat of arms of the king of Spain are engraved. And I have discovered, (much to my chagrin) that even though their stomachs are not lined with hereditary royalty, up to this very meal they have suffered no indigestion! Nor any ill effects from the wine (vino) which they drink out of crystal champagne glasses. Marvelous constitutions — n'est ce pas?

We have opened one huge ward, which has over 100 beds. The others are in the making. But this ward is so large that Dr. Barsky has put up signs on the walls to guide us. The signs read — "This way to Camp Unity," etc.

I wish you could see my laboratory. I'm very proud of it. Morris Kornblum, a technician who has just arrived a few days ago with the third American Unit, has assisted me.

I've just finished my work and am writing this letter in my lab with a 200 watt light above me to give guidance to my pen. Tonight, in the garden, where all the roses, lilies, violets, grapes, forgetmenots, irises, gladiolas, different varieties of ivy, cherry and almond blossoms are in bloom, around the swimming pool and under the huge pines, the nurses and doctors and patients and our Spanish friends are sitting and listening to the enticing music being played by Victor, our chauffeur, on his electric victrola. The entertainment is good and the moon is bright but treacherous. In our happiest moments we must fear a bright moonlight night. For it is then that we always fear and expect our uninvited guests to drop in from above. Who knows but that our expectations may come true and take form any moment or right now. For the past two days we have had a lone eagle observer. We haven't forgotten our horrible experience before. It burns in all our memories.

Well, I may move to our front line hospital soon. I'm not quite certain, but if I do I don't think I'll have much time to write. I wish, however, that you'd get all my friends to write. Even though I don't answer them, please tell them to continue to write. They must realize that I'm doing a job here, and if they were loyal to the Spanish people they would write often to us because any word from home is worth a week of relaxation. It puts us in good spirits to feel that we are not forgotten and we work harder for Spain. Once, in despair, I sat in the garden and read and reread the few scraps of mail that I had received a week before.

Please send me cigarettes. I'm dying for a good smoke. Beggars can't be choosers, but my brand is Chesterfields.

Fernanda, a Spanish nurse and my personal discovery, was sitting beside me as I wrote. She is my good man Friday. Getting ready to leave for Madrid I said to her: "Well, I'll be seeing you." She turned around and with her fiery eyes, unusually large, said, "Rosa — no agusta — yo fini — tu no amingo — yo ditha — mia abacinia — yo fini." I had a difficult time explaining that "I'll be seeing you" means hasta la vista in Spanish.

Love to all,

ROSE

Please write, and write and write!

The American Hospital Unit

LINI FUHR is of Dutch parentage, determined and self-reliant; she completed a four-year high school course in one year, graduating in 1932. In Portchester, New York, she found a job as assistant administrator of the Public Health Nursing Service. She continued her studies at night in Teachers College of Columbia University. She is a graduate nurse of the New Rochelle, N. Y., Hospital, where she later held a position as supervisor of the operating room. She was a member of the third auxiliary unit of Red Cross Nurses in which capacity she taught Girl Scout classes the first principles of nursing.

Lini Fuhr is a member of the National Association of Public Health Nurses and of the American Association of Social Workers.

March 15, 1937

Dear Ida:

The light streams across my shoulder from a small window high in the wall. I am awaiting patients to be evacuated. Just came to this hospital last night at 12 P.M. (very tired). This evidently was an old convent at one time. Now it is a pretty cold place. I have on winter underwear — sweater and my cape — still I am cold. Hated to have to leave our other hospital. It was running so well. Our house that we lived in was just rigged up with a shower and a radio the day I moved. I came last of all — now our whole medical unit is here in charge of three hospitals. Very shortly we hope to have this like our other place. Much nearer the scene of action now — a little too near for comfort — c'est la guerre —

next day — 10 A.M.
same room

Can't get accustomed to this — in our other hospital — I worked much — here I supervise the whole hospital and have others do the work — supervision is much more difficult — but it's fun — with a dictionary in one hand and the other hand for sign language I manage. Feel good today — got a whole night's sleep from 8 P.M. till 6:30 this A.M. — what to someone else a bottle of champagne may be a night's sleep and an American cigarette to us, and when we get a letter — ah — that's the height of pleasure! By the way, when are you going to write to me?

Got two letters this A.M. — one from Sadie who tells me that I got A on term paper — who cares — seems so unimportant now. Kate gave me the impression in her letter that things did not go so well in Spain. That must be the doings of the press. They will never conquer Spain.

And the Spanish people — words can't describe them — here they are in a society semi-feudalistic — yet so much higher on the thinking political level than the American people — alert, sensitive, and intelligent. I love them! My nurse Modesta came yesterday P.M. with one of our ambulances and I was glad to see her — nothing is too much for her — four weeks ago she was a peasant girl — today she gives hypos.

Just now a Negro, Frenchman, and a few Germans, Spanish and others walked in, waiting for dressings. When I speak German — anyway what I want to tell you is this — that my vocabulary is one international jumble. To go back to your question. How can I get away? We are so needed here — you cannot imagine — even if I wanted to come home — doubt if I could. And, Ida, I don't want to leave. I have the opportunity — the rare one — of working and the feeling of being valuable. Everything I have ever learned I can use here. Imagine — working and knowing every step one takes is helping these men who are fighting our fight against fascism. It no longer is work — it is — to repeat — a rare opportunity — discomforts matter not — and when one has comfort for a night or a few hours — one enjoys it more intensely. (Just gave out my last lousy Spanish cigarette) Share and share alike — comrades all.

So you are thinking — what an incoherent letter — no continuity — wish you could see me here — first the kitchen girls ask something then someone else — so on and on. But darn it I don't get thinner — a little firmer perhaps — that's all — look swell, cheeks red — five years younger (could use a bath though).

Today at two we have a gas mask drill and get our helmets — one-half block away bombs demolished the place — bloody fascists are trying to get the road my hospital is on — *They will never succeed* — We have four hospitals here.

My patients are singing near me — the French Front Populaire song. They are always asking me to sing. Don't need to join the New Singers' Chorus to express my desire to sing.

One morning from 4 A.M. till 5 A.M. I stayed with a Dutchman while he was going out. His last words were NO PASARAN. He asked me to sing to him and with tears streaming I did. One doctor accused me of being sentimental, staying with him instead of sleeping. (I had been up since six the day before.) If that's sentiment — let's have more of it. These are not ordinary soldiers dying — but going out into the struggle against fascism for you and me, for the Spanish people and the whole world. I could weep when any of them go out before my eyes.

I have seen the results of dum-dum bullets — I know what beasts the fascists are. The struggle is not 4,000 miles away, but affects everyone.

Give my love to my friends. Write soon.

LINI

↔

CHRISTOPHER CROSS volunteered as an ambulance driver and left for Spain in the early part of spring, 1937. His life has been a colorful one. From Brooklyn High School he went to the University of California in Berkeley, where he studied journalism. After that, he dug dirt for the Texas Airport, did publicity for a traveling carnival, some police reporting in the Middle West, and later wrote on a paper in Miami, Florida.

He left a position as supervisor on the Federal Writers' Project in New York City to drive an ambulance.

Villa Paz, May 12, 1937

Lou, Old Man:

I've wanted to scribble a note to you for the longest time but until now I've been in no condition to write a pal a sane letter.

On the ship, driving through France and Spain, I was just an inanimate sponge sopping up new customs, new habits; learning the real meaning of Front Populaire. I was too bewildered by the significance of it all to write. I just wanted to listen and observe.

Only yesterday, it seemed, I was going to meetings with you, plotting the continuation and expansion of W.P.A., picketing arm in arm with Helen. It took me two days to get rid of the feeling of loneliness that possessed me. This morning I made the rounds with

31

the doctors. That snapped me out of my loneliness and homesickness. The patients' greetings jolted me back to reality. I was a little ashamed of the emotions I had had.

"They say they need you very bad in Spain and greet you with all their heart," a Cuban doctor translated for a group of Spanish patients.

"I would like to shake hands with you but the fascists got my right arm and my left . . . my left is still in hock . . ."

"I used to watch for American ambulance drivers at the front. It used to make me want to fight harder. Now I can't go back to the front . . ." another said.

"Does it hurt much, comrade?" I asked.

Very slowly he removed the covers and pointed at the remaining stump of his leg.

"That's the trouble . . . I can't feel any pain . . . If I could only feel pain . . . it would bring me so much closer to our comrades who are fighting so desperately in the trenches . . . But I can't feel any pain . . . I'm numb all over . . . like that stump."

From the other side of the ward I heard, "Comrade, American Comrade, please come here."

It was Raven. I saw the hollows that were once his eyes. A fascist grenade had ripped them out. I saw a doctor examine his mutilated leg and shake his head gravely. The bones had been shattered into splinters by a fascist grenade.

"I am told, comrade, that Hemingway [New York Times correspondent in Spain who gave $40,000 of his own money and money that he borrowed, to buy ambulances for those suffering in Spain] wrote an article about me in the New York Times. I hope he told them how we're licking the fascists . . ."

"Is there something I can do for you, Raven?" I asked.

"Tell me, please, whenever you can, how things are going at the front."

"Comrade, comrade!" Raven called me back. "Is it a bright, sunny day?"

I walked out of that ward feeling myself a bigger, better man. I was sure of what I wanted and I was sure of how I was going to get it.

I chatted with Rose for more than an hour in the laboratory.

32

She's a grand person. Rose showed me your letter in which you say you have succeeded in raising fairly large sums of money. It made me very happy. That's what we need here. Money and more money to buy medical supplies, and laboratory equipment.

I chatted with Dr. Barsky a few days ago and he told me of plans to open two more hospitals. Spend two days at the front and you understand the important role of hospitals and the need for more and more. You know, of course, on what the plans for more hospitals depend. Support! Sacrifice! The majority of the workers have been giving. They must continue to give. Also we must reach the middle class. They have more to give. Continue the good work, Lou. The fight against Fascism needs mugs like you.

My fondest, warmest greetings to all my friends,

CHRIS

HOLLAND

JEF LAST was one of the first men who left his native country to go to the defense of the Spanish Government. Somewhere, in one of his letters to his wife, he tells why. He left Holland in the latter part of August 1936, before the International Brigade was thought of, when most Spaniards had to wait their turn at the front because there were no guns for them. There was, in fact, nothing that might serve them as a weapon but their bare fists. Whenever Last found time he wrote long letters to his wife, who remained behind with their three children in a dingy two-room walkup in Amsterdam's poorest section.

Although Last is the author of a number of excellent books, best known among which is "Zuider Zee," his financial resources were incredibly small, since the whole of Holland has a smaller book-reading public than the city of New York.

We are indebted to Jef Last for the most brilliant reporting of the earlier part of the Spanish struggle. His immediate and constant contact with the men in the trenches and the people of the villages has not been equaled by any other writer.

Even today Last is comparatively unknown in Spain: he is unobtrusive and makes no speeches; his life and strength are given to the struggle of the Spanish people.

October 12, 1936

There were, altogether, about twenty of us, sent out to fill in the losses of a company which had already been on the front lines for two months. Shortly before leaving Valencia, a comrade had invited us to have lunch at his house. Being an able metal worker, he could afford to live in a fairly nice little cottage. While his wife prepared the food, he showed us his vegetable garden. The little plots intended for potatoes and tomatoes were dried out and neglected. "Perdido!" This was the third time he was going to the front. No one remained behind who could work this soil. A little girl of five and a young scamp of three held tightly to their father and crept on his knee while we were eating. His wife served us with red-rimmed eyes. When we left her last words were: "No Pasaran!"

34

ar down the road we could still see her, standing on the porch of
1e house with her clenched fist high in the air.

"Our Spanish women have suffered much," said José, suddenly
ery serious — "but what can you do about it? There is no other
oad that leads to freedom!"

While we were marching to the station the comrades sang the
nternationale, the Young Guard and the Bandiera Roja. All were
ay and no one was drunk or noisy.

In between them I saw Nicasio, who is seventeen years old, and
)rubio, a farmhand from the mountains, who had to walk three
lays in order to take service with us. We have often laughed about
)rubio during those first days in the barracks: he had a hammer and
ickle shaved on his short military haircut. Only those from the
·illages could possibly think of something like that! One afternoon,
vhen I was walking with Orubio on the Avenido de la Republic, he
.uddenly started crying. He pointed to a woman who was giving the
oreast to her baby, while a little girl of about two was holding on to
1er skirts. "Mine were also three months and two years," he said,
"when the fascists came and shot them all dead. Because they refused to tell where I was hiding."

From then on nobody laughed about Orubio's hammer and sickle
coiffure any more. He himself explained it as follows: "When
the fascists get me, they will at least know that I am a Communist!"

Near the Atocha railway station they had put the diners and
sleeping cars of the International trains on the sidings. Under the
immense canopy stood only one solitary little train, ready to leave
for the front. Second class was reserved for the army men. Our
bunch took seats very carefully, as though they were visiting some
very swanky people and had to sit on the best furniture. There
wasn't a scratch on the woodwork, not the slightest spot anywhere
on the velvet upholstery. (It made me think of the large villas
which had been confiscated. One of them had been allotted to the
Women's Committee against War and Fascism, which took care
of the contributions of clothing for the soldiers who departed for
the front. There also, much to my surprise, I saw women who found
the time and who had the ambition to carefully wax the splendid
hardwood floors; and I saw how a young militia man in the hall

35

polished harness which had rusted slightly because of the w
weather.)

In the next compartment to ours a lieutenant-colonel had take
a seat in between the soldiers. He was still wearing the uniform
the old — regular army. So this was one of the "bandits." I went t
sit with him and started a conversation in French. He told me ho
he had served in Africa under Franco and Mola. "When the revol
tion broke out," he said, "back in 1931, they gave us our choice t
swear allegiance to the Republic or to be retired on full pay. Franc
swore allegiance to be that much surer of getting the entire wa
machinery of the Republic into his hands. For me, however, an oat
is an oath and a traitor a traitor. Mola had seven hundred of or
militia butchered in Toledo, seven hundred prisoners." He pointe
to the boys around us in the compartment. "Seven hundred boy
just like these. The best human material Spain ever had. And thos
people call themselves Nationalists!"

At one of the stations on the way a militia-woman got in. Spac
was made for her on our bench, there was laughing and joking, bu
no one was fresh or too free at any time. It was dark now in the com
partments. As we came into the frontlines the train went on withou
lights. Naval Peral was the last place still occupied by our forces
while behind the range of hills one could hear the barking of th
machine guns. They brought us to a confiscated country home. W
rolled ourselves in our blankets and slept as well as we could, on th
stone floor, with our knapsack as a pillow.

Today is the third day we are spending in the line of fire. Two
days ago, when we marched forward to relieve another company
we were flat on our stomachs for four long hours behind a little wal
while three enemy planes, at a comparatively low altitude, circled
around like angry wasps. The daily visit of these planes, along with
the distribution of coffee and bread in the morning, the artillery
duel which usually begins at 9 A.M., the siesta after the noon meal
and the cleaning of the weapons in the afternoon have long since
been accepted as part of our daily routine. As we do not have any
anti-aircraft guns in our sector and the planes mostly fly too high
to be within the range of our machine guns, there is nothing to do
but wait calmly until they have layed their last egg and have disappeared again behind the horizon. In these few days we have grown

36

so accustomed to them, that hardly anyone hides in the basement any more. We just stand in the door of our villa and criticize the bad marksmanship of the bombers.

Here, in the open field, with the low black wall as our only cover, it is a bit different. The feeling of complete defenselessness could easily have turned into fear if we had not seen the older comrades calmly roll their cigarettes.

High in the air and mostly invisible because of the long strings of clouds, three other planes made their appearance: our planes! Both airfleets disappeared in the mist. As though to air their disappointment, the enemy's artillery continued the bombardment with redoubled strength. Here and there above the field shrapnel exploded in poisonous little clouds. The dull thuds of the shells made one think of heavy bearpaws which were wildly clawing at us. While dusk was setting in already, we were ordered to advance to relieve the company which had occupied the first line for forty-eight hours at a stretch.

The front line positions consist of large gray boulders. Some of these are connected by breastworks of carelessly heaped up stones. Behind us, far below, lies Naval Peral, where the shells are constantly exploding in bouquets of whirled-up dust and stones. In front of us, on the high crests of the mountains which enclose the village, lie the Moors, also invisible behind their boulders. Twice already the village has been in their hands. Twice the column of Mangada has recaptured it from the enemy. Now they are trying for the third time to close the iron ring around us, which right now is only broken by a narrow opening where the armored train continually rides back and forth over the rails. In the meantime this ring has become so narrow that the spot where we are lying is not only under the fire from the enemy in front of us, but also gets many of the accidental bullets from the left and right flanks.

This is already the third day that we are lying here and still there is not a single act of heroism that can be told of our company. After the big bombardment of Sunday, when the enemy pumped more than two thousand shells into our village, the staff expected an attack of Moorish cavalry, and we pierced tensely ahead into the night. Comrades said: "Be sure that you always save *one* bullet. When the Moors take us prisoners we are not only shot but they

37

cut us to pieces with their bayonets while alive." The flaps of our cartridge belts were open and our hands were on our triggers, but the anticipated attack was not forthcoming. There was a rumor abroad that the Moors, suffering from the cold, had refused to attack. Later in the night, like mad dogs, the barking of the machine guns would break out repeatedly on other sectors of the front. Near us, now and again, lost bullets would whistle past like angry wasps. Or they would bite with a dry smack into the stones of our breastwork. Our real enemy was not those bullets, but cold and rain. That whole first night the rain came down, incessantly, in streams. The tension fell somewhat and only the sentinel stood guard while we were shivering on the glistening wet stones, wrapped only in our single blankets. When day came, dirty, gray masses of clouds crept slowly nearer from behind the mountains in the west. Lost streamers from the main body of the clouds enclosed us again and again for long minutes in their ice-cold mist. Not for one single moment did the sun break through. After twenty-four hours shoes and socks were soaked through and our blankets weighed like lead on our shoulders. Warm food did not arrive, as the enemy artillery had chased a few shells right into the middle of our field-kitchen. The second day, when the enemy took our line of communication with the village under fire, bread, sausage and wine stopped coming too. This morning our sergeant crept through the line of fire on his stomach, and came back with a small barrel of wine and a few bunches of grapes. Each of us only got a half a mug though, "because," say the boys, "if you drink much on an empty stomach, you can't shoot straight any more."

Little Nicasio calmly walks back and forth on the level as though the bullets weren't whistling any closer over our heads than they did yesterday and cuts thistles with his bayonet. We make a poor little fire with these behind the largest boulder. It gives more smoke than warmth . . .

That morning at eleven o'clock the captain came by. "We must try to stick it out until five o'clock tonight! All reserves are needed for the other sectors, where the enemy is attacking constantly. I can only replace those who feel absolutely sick!"

No one reported. In our completely drenched blankets we hunched behind the rocks and Jésus Martin Perez, a street cleaner

om Madrid, who was lying next to me, said: "That's not so bad,
placement at five o'clock already. Fourteen days ago we were like
us on the rocks for eight days in a row, and three of them without
anything to eat."

I think it cannot be stressed enough that all our militiamen, with-
ut a single exception, are volunteers, and that our regiments are
othing but party-formations with weapons. From the tenth of
ctober on, the militarization will begin. On that date the unity of
ommand will be instituted under the war ministry, simultaneously
ith the new, democratic, but stern military discipline.

Fully confident of the determination of these people to be victori-
us, the government leaves it up to anyone who does not accept this
ilitarization to break his enlistment pledge and to go home on
he tenth of October. And that in the middle of the war!

Most of the men in our company have already been on the front
or two months, without a single day's furlough. Their pay is more
han a month in arrears. How will they react?

We were replaced that afternoon by a company that had only
rrived from Madrid a few hours ago. Practically all of them were
olunteers, who came to the front for the first time. Not only in
ge but in all their ways they had something of children about them.
hey took our guns over and we saw their last rows disappear be-
ind the top of the hill, singing the stanza: "Sabemos vencer o
uerir" (We know how to conquer or to die), from the "Young
uard." This song was to them something more than merely a
logan.

Without weapons we remained behind in our villa as reserves.
rom the room in the tower we could follow the entire operations
f the next day. The enemy began a desperate offensive and suc-
eeded in closing the only road that connects us with Madrid for
everal hours. Only our captain had a revolver. Our boys said
iercely: "If they break through now the Moors will still get us
live!" A new aerial attack was announced from the north.

At that moment the sergeants came to announce that our political
delegate would speak on the meaning of militarization in the hall on
he main floor. Five minutes later the Moors and the flyers above
ur heads were forgotten. The all-consuming convictions flamed
p in the discussions. There were farmhands who could not under-

39

stand the difference between capitalist and democratic disciplin
They said: "We have been soldiers under the king and we onl
fight as volunteers in order that our children may not have to l
soldiers." Others said: "Even though they order us to ten times, w
will still refuse to shoot comrades on orders from above, just b
cause of some dumb mistake of theirs."

Deeper and sounder were the objections of the anarchists. Jésu
formulated: "We are the armed people, the fighters of the revolu
tion, and we will not be reduced to will-less troops of the goverr
ment."

Our delegate pointed out that the syndicalists had also realize
the necessity of an iron discipline in their newspapers. He said tha
the cooperation and control of the party gave the guarantee tha
the troops would not be misused. He pointed out that our losse
until now had been ten times as high as would have been necessar
under military discipline and decent military training. He stresse
the necessity of a victory, which, against the well-drilled troops o
the rebels, would only be possible by a strict submission to on
single military leadership.

Without having reached a definite decision the gathering brok
up. Three days later our company returned on leave to Madrid
Those who were in agreement with the militarization, could repor
at the barracks two days later. This morning on the exercise ground
I have seen all of them back again: Orubio, José, Nicasio, and Jésus
who was the spokesman for the anarchists. One after the other w
received our new books. Jésus greeted me in the fashion of the
anarchists by encircling the wrist of one by the hand of the other
He laughed: "We have been *one* company and we are going to re
main together. Most important is victory."

So probably we will go back to the front in a day or two witl
these same "bandits." They tell us that there is snow already in th
Sierras.

Madrid, October 20th, 1936

Certainly the town has changed! I knew the Gran Via and the
Calle Alcala, with its pretentious skyscrapers and even more pretentious show of swanky automobiles. The blasé distinction of the

ternational hotels, the boulevards where one sauntered, and the
fés where time itself had stopped over the endless conversations,
the blue mist of cigarette smoke. I knew — in the subway, on
e steps of banks, hotels, and theatres — in the parks and in front
the churches — the invalids, the beggars, and the mothers who
ploited the misery of their children. I knew the horror of the poor
ctions and the glistening tricornes of the *gardes civilos* which made
e think of lacquered coffins.

The beggars had disappeared, however, together with the civil
ard. The luxurious automobiles have been confiscated, and are
inted over roughly with red and white letters. The bored, saun-
ring bourgeoisie has been swept from the street. Instead the
reets are black with uniforms, or rather — who can speak of uni-
rms here! — they are black with workers in overalls, who are
sily recognized as militiamen by their cap; a cartridge belt with a
volver and a gun slung over their shoulder. They are the ones
ho give the town its new appearance; the unmistakable proletarian
ght of the Revolution!

In Nawas del Marques we suddenly got orders in the middle of
e night to help in the moving of several pieces of a field-battery.
e worked like horses through the water-soaked fields. Next to me
the line were a student of architecture, an art teacher, and an
countant. The commander of the battery was a mathematics
ofessor who had studied in Berlin.

"When the 'rebellion' started," he told me, "we had practically
ot one single commissioned officer in the artillery. In these few
onths we have been forced to train an entirely new body from
athematicians and intellectuals."

And what has all this to do with the cultural aspect of Madrid?
De Alvarez said to me: "To us it is a very simple question. It is
ot only a question of 'conquer or die.' But when we die every hope
es with us, for progress, for everything that makes it worthwhile
live. On our side stands everything that is art, intellect and
manism in Spain. On the other side the most conceited, ignorant
ourgeoisie, the most impudent landowners and the most illiterate
ergy that the world has ever known. That is why this fight cannot
d while there are still ten people alive who really love Spain.
lways the opposition will rise again."

From Spanish Trenches

I am thinking of the nervous spiritual figure of Bergamin, tl
well-known Catholic philosopher and writer. There is somethir
wooden about his movements, that makes one think every now ar
then of an invalid. In reality he is a constant source of energy ar
inspiration. Alberti said of him: "Bergamin is the bravest of us all

In one of the little restaurants of Madrid I speak with Bergam
about several Dutch young Catholics I have known. He constant
asks new questions and I feel that here there is a hunger for know
edge that I cannot satisfy: here in front of me sits someone wl
calls into the desert and listens, listens, if the call of the broth
does not answer from somewhere behind the horizon.

"I know," says Bergamin, "that the social rebirth of Catholicis
is every bit as necessary as the spiritualization of a Communis
which without this must sink down into a morass of opportunism.
know that communion and communism have the same roots, an
that regardless of appearances our hearts have already found eac
other, because all others desire righteousness for the humble of tl
earth: for those who are closest to Jesus Christ. It is not an accider
that the Apostles of Christ were laborers and not generals lil
Mola!"

Not in the armed fist of Mola but in the slight writer's hand of
Bergamin are the deepest treasures of Catholicism preserved. An
Bergamin, of whom we are proud, stands on the side of the simp
militiamen who fight in the mountains for a reborn Spain.

Bergamin is the son of one of the best known lawyers of Madri
who was a conservative minister under the reign of the king. H
also studied law. His feeling of right and wrong is linked irresistibl
to his deep Catholic conviction of life. Next to me at the little ca
table sits the man, who, when consulted by the government as
Catholic, declared himself *against* the re-opening of the churches i
Madrid: "Rather the catacombs, at least, that is real. The questio
of Catholicism in Spain is too deep to be satisfied with a purely o
portunistic solution for the sake of propaganda. *It is not a questio
of the opening or closing of churches but of the pure revival of the tr
Catholicism in the hearts.*" Only the man who three years ago a
ready put into the title of his magazine the program of the irrevo
cable battle for unity can speak in this way. This magazine wa
called: "Cruz Y Raya," which in Spanish is a play of words difficu

42

o translate. It means "Tabula Rasa" as well as "Plus and Minus," or "Yes and No!" Cruz Y Raya developed from a literary review into a publishing house that brought out everything which in itself had a deeper human value according to the opinion of Bergamin. Cruz Y Raya published Malraux and Alberti as well as the great Spanish mystics. Cruz Y Raya brought out the young Spanish and Spanish-American poets simultaneously with a biography of St. Catherine of Sienna, the studies of Bergamin about Lope de Vega and new editions of the great Spanish classics.

In a short time Cruz Y Raya became the center in which all the streets of Spanish intellect came together; a source of revolutionary energy on all the fields of spiritual life.

Not that it concerned itself with politics in the ordinary meaning of the word. "When I invited a physicist to write about physics or a musician about music," says Bergamin, "I did not ask myself if his political convictions agreed with mine. So great is my conviction that all real science, all real art and all true religion result in the end in the same thing: service to humanity."

In "Las Cosas Claras," citations from the great Spanish thinkers and poets — Bergamin tried to point out this unity of human endeavor as the red thread that runs through the entire Spanish — yes — through the entire culture of the world: "The great tradition of Spain has always been revolutionary. Every system of thought is built up dialectically of two oppositions: the conservative wish for maintenance of age old groups and the revolutionary tendency which strives for a constant advance in the contemporary field. Our classics were great because they were constantly in living contact with the people, and here in Spain the word "people" has the connotation "revolution." Bergamin sees in this humanism the base that can become — over the borders of political parties — the foundation for a united front that is not only opportunistic.

"Man is everywhere," he says, "and everything is for man. I am a Christian because God became in Christ a man like myself. If we did not see God in man, it would be impossible for us to have true communion with Him. But still it is possible for Christians and non-Christians to find each other in this belief in man. *The purpose of Christianity is the rebirth of man*, but is it not remarkable that I can only speak with Communists nowadays about the 'New Man'.

From Spanish Trenches

Nietszche, hostile though he otherwise was toward Christianity, sought in his 'Uebermensch' only this new man, the same one that we want also, the same one who, in another form, is the constantly recurring subject of the newer Russian literature. This literature is related to our way of thinking. Just because it — just as we — believe that every human being already carries the possibility of this 'New Man' in himself.

"There are, however, other things that unite us.

"From far back humanity knows the implications of the term 'race'. Literally 'race' means: *trace*. The trace of the blood that continues through the times. They who make race their deity — as the Nazis today — are the slaves of the inheritance of blood. But Jesus Christ came just in order to release us through His blood of this inheritance. He gave His blood to show that blood is *not* the highest. Therefore Christianity teaches that faith will become blood to us. Faith, however, and the spirit are one. In the Catholic church the sacrament is to some extent 'materialistic' and therefore I state with pleasure that a Christian cannot be an idealist in a philosophic sense, but that historical materialism is much closer to us than is generally accepted.

"I interest myself as a Catholic in every thinker and reformer who seriously seeks the road to make man's life more humane. And even though we are separated on many planes of thought I still make the words of Malraux mine: 'We can always agree on life, even though our thoughts differ on death!'"

What part of the Spanish people, I asked Bergamin, had he been able to reach through the medium of Cruz Y Raya?

Readily he admits: "Only a very small minority of intellectuals. Our paper had a circulation of 1700 copies, of which even then a large part still went to America. The official world, the great press, and the clergy ignored us as though we did not exist, which is worse than active opposition. Furthermore, it is impossible to think of a bourgeoisie in Europe whose spiritual life was on such a low level as it was in Spain. What has pleased me more than anything else is the understanding that I, with my action, have constantly found the sympathy of the simple and unlettered among our common people.'

When Bergamin speaks about the people, his cheeks begin to glow and his face takes on an almost ecstatic expression. For him

people are not what they are to the Fascists: a dull mass of low
manity kept in bondage by a small group of rulers; for him the
ple are the chaos from which a new world is born, the unfathom-
le reservoir of forces from which every thinker and poet, who
es not want to be shut off from life, must draw.

I asked Bergamin which place the Church as an organization
ıld take in this system of his, which always again puts the simple
man being of the masses ahead.

"But," answered Bergamin, almost naively, "what is the Church
t the people itself, the community of all those who believe in the
ristian truth? Not separately, but only in community can man
lize Christian righteousness here on earth."

The thoughts of Bergamin are to me ideas from a completely
ferent spiritual world than the one in which I am accustomed to
e. The undying conviction and the noble soul of Bergamin, how-
er, are the same which I have learned to know of the best Com-
nists of our time. If placed before a judge, Bergamin would also
tify like a Dimitroff. The conversation with Bergamin has
engthened my conviction that unsurmountable imaginary con-
dictions are perhaps less deep than we originally thought them to
and that Fascism, with the harm that it has created in the
rld, perhaps has this one good point, that it brings the best
rits from all progressive parties ever closer and closer in the same
tle for a new and happier humanity."

Madrid, November 18, 1936

The reasons for our retreat at Getafe are deeply rooted, and per-
es they are partly inevitable in a struggle like this, where an army
not been built up systematically over a period of years, but has
ruth been improvised by the proletariat. On top of that come
specific political circumstances in Spain. The contrast between
Anarchists and the Communists and the fear of both groups
t the other might make a grab for power has been the reason for
ning officers everywhere not because they were composed of the
t military material, but because they were those who could best
rusted from the political point of view. While the fight was going
promotions were made on the basis of proven bravery, which is,

however, in many cases, quite different from military clearsighte
ness or organizational ability. Our Captain, for example, is a mo
charming boy of twenty who has had one and a half years of schoo
ing, worked in a factory at the age of nine, participated in his fir
strike at eleven, got his first jail sentence at fifteen and who ev
since did wonderful work in the illegal Youth Movement. He
brave, has a good disposition, a lot of good will, but in reality he
nothing but a big child, without authority or military foresigl
That our men are brave, one and all, was proven sufficiently
Naval Peral and on other occasions, but in the first place they a
big children, who never look ahead, and in the second place they a
so anarchistic and anti-militaristic in their deepest being, that th
greet every effort to bring more military discipline into the troo
with suspicion. It is true, of course, that the political commissa
have done good work here, and the unity of command is constant
being enforced more rigidly, but they are still very far away fr
being a red army. In addition to all this, our company had the b
fortune to get replacements from the village, men who had nev
been under fire before.

At eight o'clock in the evening, the order came that we were
advance and until two o'clock in the morning there was singing a
laughing as though they were going to a party instead of to t
trenches. I must add to this, that all drinking was forbidden on su
occasions in the barracks, so that there can be no question of drur
enness. As far as that is concerned, the boys will warn you the
selves: "Careful, when you have been drinking, you can't sho
straight."

At two in the morning our buses departed and at the first gr
light of morning we replaced the First and Fourth companies in
trenches. These trenches themselves belong to the fortifications
Madrid. They have been constructed in all haste by the wom
the boys and the workers who are too old to carry arms, in th
spare time. From the military point of view, they are complet
inadequate, so narrow that the officers cannot pass through fre
They have no ridge to rest the arms on, on which one can also
cartridges. They are without drainage in rainy weather, and wo
of all, they have no dug-outs where the men can seek shelter agai
wind and cold. So here again we find typical improvisation.

46

When the sun went up, we found out that there was a second line
of soldiers about three hundred yards ahead of our position in the
field.

It was beautiful weather, almost summer, the batteries were
silent and we almost had the feeling of being in the country on a
little outing — for our health. I studied Spanish industriously from
a little handbook which I had bought. A squadron of planes bombarded the first line, but left us in peace. Only the commissary func-
ioned badly. That whole day and the next one we got nothing to
eat but some dry bread and a piece of sausage. In the afternoon a
car came by with some women from the World-Committee. They
old us that the first line was pretty much demoralized because of
the bombardment. They distributed a few bottles of Cognac. I had
a long conversation with two nurses from the Scottish Ambulance
Unit, who do some swell work. The night was freezing cold, but we
had found some straw in a barn and slept fairly comfortably under
our blankets. It was hilly, so I was not able to see the line to the
right of the road. Since it seemed the next morning as though the
day would pass again in complete calm, our captain went to Madrid
to get blankets and clothes for the men.

At eleven o'clock, suddenly, intense rifle fire started in the first
line, and toward one we saw the troops from that line fall back in a
fairly orderly manner. We brought them to a stand. The officers
ordered them back into our trench. This was the first big mistake.
Because of this, the trench became overfilled, with demoralized
forces at that. What should have been done, of course, was to have
them form in a third line behind ours, as a protection for the village.
At about two o'clock, the big play started. The enemy opened up a
big bombardment on our line, which lasted for more than two
hours without a let-up. In addition to that, five tanks, or rather
armored cars, rode up and down along the highway and peppered
us incessantly with machine gun fire. We ourselves had only an
armored train at our disposal, and a junky armored car on the road,
both of which had to draw back pretty soon. Our machine guns
dated from the Middle Ages and hitched constantly. It was remarkable that regardless of all this, the enemy's fire did but little damage in our trench. What was much worse was that our boys were
constantly firing when there was even no enemy in sight. (The

47

armored cars were immune to our bullets, of course.) On top of al
that, most of them shot without taking aim, so that the bullet
would often hit the ground no more than thirty yards from ou
line. As a result munitions began to run short everywhere towar
evening and many guns became unclear. I tried, as much as I coulc
to hold the firing, in which I succeeded fairly well in our section, bu
my voice, of course, did not reach much further than a hundre
yards. Then came the attack. As the tanks were not able to brea
through on our sector, they went to the right of the highway an
there they succeeded in breaking through the lines in two places a
about four o'clock. At that moment a panic ensued on the extren
right wing and one of the companies ran for dear life. That on
company dragged along the others: especially those soldiers wh
had no ammunition any more or whose guns did not function. The
left the line without any order. The officers commanded them t
hold their positions, but a feeling of comradeship evidently kej
them from shooting at the fugitives, although the retreat migl
have been stopped that way. The breach became wider and wid
and then the retreat started to the left of us, too. In my section
held the men as long as I could with words and sometimes l
threatening them with my gun. We held out a quarter of an ho
longer than the others, perhaps, but at last I was all alone in tl
trench with our *alvarez* (second lieutenant), who had come ba
when I called him a coward. "*Somos solos,*" [We are alone] he sai
At that moment the enemy was at about three hundred yards.
saw that nothing could be done so I ran with him in the direction
Getafe. At a railroad crossing we found a few officers and for a f
minutes we formed a second line of defense with them, but th
position became impossible to hold also. We saw the lines of t
fascists coming toward us slowly against the sinking sun. My thro
was dry as leather. All out of breath, we dragged a box of ammu
tion along the road. Pretty soon we had to leave that behind
order to carry a wounded man. His blood streamed over my han
and he was constantly wailing: "An auto, an auto." At last
found an ambulance; it had become completely dark in the mea
time. I rested up in a house halfway to Madrid. Perhaps a half
hour later we were chased out by an alarm. On the road stoo
company of our Assaltos. (These are not volunteers, but regu

48

roops.) I asked them something and evidently they took me for a spy or for a fascist, who had walked too far ahead by accident. This was the most horrible moment of that night, because they stood there, guns raised to shoot me. Luckily I could prove with my papers that everything was okay. I attached myself to them and marched back in the direction of Getafe where we occupied a position on the road with about a hundred men. There we lay the entire following morning, without reinforcements and with no other food than the raw tomatoes which grew in the field. I thought: "This will be the end if they attack. Notwithstanding this, the exhaustion had been so great that I fell asleep in a ditch along the road. I awakened by being shaken by someone and at once I saw the kind, good-hearted face of our Sergeant Rubio before me. He had come back to the line of fire, searching for me. I think that never in my life have I been so happy. With him I found our company back in Madrid.

That same evening we marched with our newly-formed company to Villa Verde Bajo, where we got the order to protect an artillery battery, which had been placed there. While part of our company went into the trenches, the rest of us were housed in the oven of a brick-yard, the most fantastic performance you could possibly imagine. Because of the heat, we fell asleep immediately, but hardly two hours later the artillery changed its position and we moved to the basement of a sort of castle, in the tower of which the lookout of the artillery had been placed. It was hardly day when the enemy got wise to this and pretty soon it rained shells. We were ordered to retreat behind the embankment of a railroad. Since half of our company had no cartridges any more, Peppe did not know what he should do. I advised him to send back to Madrid all those who had little or no cartridges left and to advance with the rest.

He tried it too, but did not have enough authority to put it over. At that moment something terrible happened, somewhere along the front a second break occurred and whole troops of fleeing men came in our direction. I understood that this was a panic and that it was not a case of real danger and I tried to induce Peppe to march forward with our company in order to stem the enemy's advance, whereupon a corporal suggested to me that we should advance ourselves in the hope that the others would follow.

From Spanish Trenches

No more than about six, however, came along. We advanced about four kilometers with our small contingent through fields and over deserted trenches, until at last we found a detachment of about forty men on the Cadiz road who were defending this transportation line. They were terribly happy that we had come and that whole afternoon we succeeded in keeping the enemy outside of Villa Verde Alto by our fire. Toward evening reinforcements arrived and the commander gave us permission to retreat and to find our own company. That evening was perhaps even more horrible than the last one. Wherever we passed we found lost groups of militiamen, without weapons and without munitions, hungry, without officers, not knowing where to go. The railroad which we followed had been bombarded and the station was one smoking ruin. Dozens of airplanes circled against the blood-red sky. They constantly swooped down along the fields where they decimated the fleeing militiamen with machine gun fire. Their bombs fell like hail and everywhere we looked we could see high columns of smoke and flames reaching up over the villages.

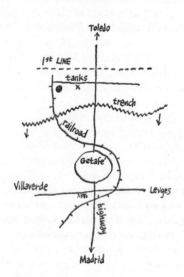

In a few minutes only one burning mass was left where the model garden village of the railroad workers had been. Fermin, who had been with me all day, said: "Madrid is taken," and even I believed at that moment that there was nothing left to do but to chase a bullet through my head, yet the urge to live was greater and furthermore, I had gathered up a whole bunch of the boys from our company who had lost their heads. With them I formed a small division, with which I marched back as quickly as possible to our barracks at the Puente de Vallecas to ask for new orders. The Commandant considered what I told him of such importance, that he immediately brought me to headquarters in an automobile. To my pleasure, I noticed that there, at least, they had not gone berserk quite as much as I had expected. It is true that the breach made by the fascists was very serious, but since it took place only over a very small front, it became at the same time dangerous for them because they practically found themselves in a bottle-neck.

After they had heard at the staff what I had to tell, they supplied me with a good bath and the first warm food in four days, so I returned to the barracks like a new man. The next day Domela and the others came back to the barracks, too. That night they had defended the same road we had been on in the afternoon.

It probably will sound strange, but the quiet days which followed were the worst of all. Our company occupied a trench behind the Manzanares River but in the meantime the enemy had changed the direction of its attack more to the south, toward the Casa de Campo. Only the artillery and the planes were constantly at us. It seemed as though they were after us, because two shells crashed into the breastwork of our trench, another one at not more than a yard from the place where Domela, Peppe, and I were squatting. We were completely covered with dirt, and it is the mere chance that it did not explode that explains the fact that I am still able to write to you. Hardly five minutes later an *escadre* of planes came our way, and when I saw tens of bombs coming right at us from above like white eggs, I thought that everything was finished. But they were carried away by the wind and exploded about twenty yards away from us. This is not what I mean when I say: "the worst," though, because all of this is merely part of the war.

About two hundred yards behind our lines, lies one of those hor-

51

rible slums of Madrid, without sewerage or plumbing of any sort
The love with which we were received in this neighborhood canno
be described. A little old grandmother carried us her last loaf o
bread and her last little bit of wine ——

Telephone, report immediately at barracks, leaving for front.

November 24, 1936

So we are at the front again, but such a front. You could no
imagine anything more fantastic, hardly eight minutes walking
distance from the "Cuatro Caminos" subway station. Transporta
tion of our company to the front was extremely simple this time
we just took the subway. But at the same time you will be able to
understand how terribly dangerous the advance of the fascists was
It literally brought them to the gates of Madrid, even though it was
only in the form of a wedge, so that their front is very narrow here.

Our company is housed in a deserted roadhouse. When they
have relief periods from the firing line, our militiamen play with the
marble game, or they turn on the electric piano, and practice bull-
fighting with crazy-looking overcoats, using some cow horns
mounted on some sort of a little wagon as their antagonist! In front
of us lies University City, where the Republican government was
building a model city with tremendous hospitals, schools, student
houses, stadiums and parks, partly to provide work for the
unemployed. It was meant as a fortress of culture, and human
endeavor, but Franco has made a fortress of the hospitals and
university buildings, from which he destroys culture and life in
Madrid. It is from this city that we are driving the enemy away
systematically but slowly, and here the International Brigade is
doing especially marvellous work.

When I had to break off my last letter suddenly, I was just going
to write to you about the worst which I have seen here, and that is
the incredible and unnecessary suffering of the non-combatants.
It is clear that the enemy does not concentrate on attacking points
of strategic importance, but that they throw most of their bombs
and shells exclusively on the workers' districts. With this refined
method of torture they hope to drive them through fear to panic.

I wrote to you about slums behind our lines, where only the poor-

st of the poor live, and how they came carrying the last of their
ittle possessions to take care of us. Their few sad-looking chickens,
heir blankets, their mattresses, their tomatoes — they wanted to
;ive us everything. They sewed on buttons for us, washed our
;lothes, took care of us as though we were their own children. Of
:ourse you can rest assured that we did not want to endanger them
»y quartering troops in their section, our trenches were at least
hree hundred yards further on, but the enemy's fliers bombarded
heir poor huts with sadistic pleasure. In our trench we could hear
he terrible cries of agony of the victims. Later we carried from the
uins the little dead bodies of the children who the previous day sat
»n our laps, and the mutilated bodies of the women who had taken
:are of us. In Puente Vallecas the bombs tore off the whole front of
)ne of those tenements so that one could see the poverty gouging
)ut like the intestines of a horse that had its stomach ripped open
by the horns of a bull. On the Puerta del Sol, the busiest square of
the town, the bombs went through the street into the subway station. The Don Carlos Hospital was hit by incendiary bombs, the
gorgeous Liria Palace, one of the most beautiful museums, was
completely destroyed; every day the city would go into hiding behind clouds of smoke and every night the sky would be a burning
red.

Those who lie in the trenches at least have a gun in their hands,
that gives them the illusion that they can defend themselves, but in
the city you can do nothing but wait for the next bomb to fall, perhaps on your own house, on your own family! There is no end to all
this horror. As soon as the sun shines, twenty, and sometimes
thirty or forty enemy planes will circle over the town and drop their
bombs. When it gets cloudy, the enemy's batteries will sling their
incendiary bombs into the town, hoping they will hit a good target.
Under these circumstances, I can think of no more derisive epithet
than the word "world-conscience." Even the hordes of Attila did
not destroy their own capital, nor did they use their weapons to
butcher the women and children of their own people.

I wrote needless — and meant really useless cruelties. The enemy
can destroy Madrid, but he cannot terrorize it. These people are
more than admirable, they take interest in an aerial battle in very
much the same way as they used to watch a bullfight. At two hun-

From Spanish Trenches

dred yards from the "Ciné Monumental" bombs score a hit and
destroy the whole neighborhood, but in the theatre the performance continues uninterrupted. Street cars and subways run as usual,
the cafés are filled, children play soccer or soldier. Nobody thinks
of giving up. On the contrary, everybody who has two hands works
from early to late building barricades in the streets. If Franco
wants to penetrate into Madrid, he will have to capture it house for
house and alley for alley.

While I am writing the captain establishes the fines of those who
have been caught playing cards. Playing cards is not cultural, because one takes away the money from another's pocket! The fines
go into the fund of the International Red Cross! That is the way
things are with the barbarians!

December 10, 1936, Frente de L'Estacion de Goya

The position which we occupy here — the Goya Station Front —
is in one of the suburbs of Madrid. It consists of a group of tenements. Holes have been broken through the walls, in order to connect them by trenches. When there is no fighting, all those who
have no sentinel duty live and sleep in these houses which offer a
fairly good protection against gun and shrapnel fire. Since it is
getting colder right along, we make a fire in a bucket on the cement
floor. We have to be very careful that the smoke is not visible to the
enemy, because they would take us under fire immediately. So we
close doors, windows and chimney, with the result that the room is
so full of smoke that you can cut it. At night we sleep in that same
smoke, in all our clothes, shoes laced and cartridge belt around the
waist. You can understand that this did not help my bronchitis
much. My voice is practically gone, especially since I have yelled
too much giving orders during night fighting in the last few days.
Yesterday I felt so rotten, that I went to see the doctor. He gave
me a can of condensed milk and told me to drink it with some cognac, as hot as I could stand it. In addition to that I was relieved
from duty for the night and put in my eight hours for the first time
in I don't know how long, without my clothes on and under a few
decent blankets. The next morning I felt much better, but Peppe
told me to stick around the telephone which connects us with head-

54

quarters. He would take my place in the front line. You owe it to his comparative house-arrest that I am writing.

I was just talking over the telephone and while I am looking at he instrument it is almost as though it were the symbol of all the shortcomings which we will have to conquer before we arrive at the big offensive and the final victory. When the enemy — four weeks ago now — broke through our lines first at Getafe and then at Villa Verde I thought for just one moment — and I was not the only one who thought this — that everything was lost. I had seen the disorganized companies being decimated by the machine gun fire of low swooping Heinkels. From villages and stations which we passed the flames flared high into the air, then the buildings would cave in under shell fire. Moorish cavalry sabred down whatever they met. They chased our troops way back to the Princeses Bridge and the Franceses Bridge, which cross the Manzanares. I maintain that it was the women who saved Madrid in those despairing days. They chased the men, who had fled to their homes, back to the front, or they picked up the guns which the men had thrown away in their haste and themselves defended the city behind barricades which had been thrown together hurriedly. It soon became evident that the fleeing of the militiamen was not the result of cowardice, but could only be considered as a typical panic. They who had fled in the past few days streamed back to their companies and not only showed resistance, but started the counter-offensive, under circumstances many times more difficult.

They succeeded — with enormous sacrifices and unlimited bravery — in definitely stemming the advance of the enemy; even in winning back several of the important positions. I repeat what I have already written: our militiamen are the finest and bravest human material you can imagine, providing they are well led. In many ways they are just like children, extremely susceptible to psychic contagion when strong leadership is lacking, or if the officers lose their heads. When they come to their senses later they are ready to show the most crazy courage because they are ashamed of themselves and want to make up for it. The days of Getafe and Villa Verde are also the days in which boys like Col captured enemy tank after enemy tank, with nothing but a few hand grenades. That Saturday Franco announced over the radio that he would drink his coffee in Madrid the next day. Radio-Lissabon described how he had triumphantly entered the city on a white horse. In Avila the blood-tribunal, which was to take over the reign of the city, had already been named. Foreign correspondents were forbidden to follow the army, Franco wanted to be alone when he settled with the inhabitants of Madrid. Mola counted on a repetition of Badajoz and announced the penalty of death for anyone who might be found with weapons. . . That was four weeks ago. In the meantime Franco's coffee has become cold! All of them miscalculated because they did not understand the proletariat and because they did not know that even though this proletariat may make mistakes, it learns from those mistakes; that you can beat it down, but that it will get up again every time, that it can fall back for a moment, but then only to resume the battle with so much more courage and conviction. In their haste they bumped their heads into a bloody mess, against the renewed heroism of the people of Madrid.

To come back to that telephone.

Our position partly depends for its defense on an armored train which can come from Madrid within a few minutes in case of a heavy attack. In order to be able to call this train at a minute's notice, a field telephone was installed in all haste. When it was installed and when the workmen had gone back it turned out that a contact was missing somewhere, so that it would not work. For more than three days we were there before a repair man at last came who re-established the contact. During all that time the men amused themselves royally with the telephone . . . which did not work. The captain, the *alvarez*, the sergeants, and everybody who came into headquarters, played telephone. They called up their fiancee, their mother-in-law, they ordered a supper with champagne in the city, or they held fabricated conversations with Mola and Queipo de Llano, whose hides they covered with insults. To me the telephone seemed the reflection of their greatest worth as well as of their greatest weakness; their joyous lack of worry, which always keeps them gay and full of good humor, but through which they also, only too often, neglect the most necessary action at a moment when there still is time!

The enemy lies in a trench at about eight hundred yards from us. This trench runs from the military hospital to the Estremadura

ighway. Opposite us they occupy a little village and we can very
clearly see the holes in the houses, where they have mounted their
machine guns. The artillery base, which puts us under fire for several hours every afternoon, must be just beyond that. They shoot
badly and most of their projectiles explode one hundred yards behind our line on the cemetery, where they seem to begrudge the
dead their rest. Or is it possible that the fascist motto "Spain,
Awake!" is meant for them too?

Still the war has pretty badly damaged the workers' houses,
which together with the trench form our line. Everywhere holes
have been hacked into the walls. We shoot through them when
there is an attack. The moon looks in through the broken tiles in the
roof, the windows are broken and replaced by boards which keep
the light out. In the evening, the flame of a wick floating in turbid
oil makes the dark shadows of the broken furniture look spooky.
From the wall a bridal couple stares at us from a gold frame which
is almost hidden by cobwebs. A broken gramophone is proof of a
modest attempt at prosperity. Two of the boys are busy cutting up
an old high chair for fire wood.

A bunch of books are swept together in a corner. Everything is
filthy, dusty, broken and neglected. In the houses a little way up
you can hear the hoarse howling of the hungry dogs, who were left
behind.

We have already been living in these ruins twelve days. Everything we touch is filthy, even the water from the well is muddy and
leaves grey dregs in our mugs. It is too cold to wash with, decently.
The stoop in front of our house — the only piece of road which is
not in the line of fire — is unapproachable because of the excretions
of one hundred and forty soldiers. For twelve days we haven't been
out of our clothes, three times we have thrown the enemy back
after a night attack, every day we stand at our posts for eight
hours, most of us don't even have decent shoes, and at no time during these two weeks have we had a hot meal, since the field kitchen
can't get through.

Yet during all these weeks I have not heard a single complaint.
At night, when we sit around the fire with tears streaming down
our faces, the comrades tell stories! Tyl Eulenspiegel or Ali Baba
and the Forty Thieves. There is a lot of singing, too. Nobody

57

doubts our victory. Yesterday a bullet shattered the shoulder blade of our little Manuelo. Thomas has been hit in the thigh by a splinter of shrapnel. "*Que suerte!*" say the comrades, "What luck! Not a single one of us killed in this whole week!"

Often they ask me: "Tell us again, *teniente*, why did you really come here!" I shrug my shoulders: "Well, boys, you ought to know that story by now, because your battle is our battle, too!" "Yes," they say, "we know that, but he over there comes from the village, you must explain it carefully for him once more!" I get my map and point out how France is surrounded on all sides by the fascists if they should come to win in Spain. With Spain to bolster it, Germany can shut off England from its colonies. That will be the moment when a new world war will have to break out, under the most favorable circumstances for fascism. For that reason we are not only defending Spain, but Democracy and even the borders of the Soviet Union!

They look at me with shining eyes and say: "*Que lucha!* Boy, what a battle!"

Several times during the last few weeks we have witnessed aerial combats. The fleet, which went in the direction of Madrid over our positions, was the largest I have ever seen. Thirty-nine gigantic bombers, protected by twenty pursuit planes. They don't take the trouble any more these days to bombard the trenches, knowing how extremely difficult it is to hit a narrow line like that. Without bothering about the troops, they take a straight course for Madrid, which offers them a much surer target. The town, which has but little charm once one is in it, looks, as seen from our position, like a phantasmagorical fairy city on the hills. Then the planes approach, the earth rumbles from the dull sound of the explosions and five minutes later the whole town has disappeared in dirty brown clouds of dust and smoke; even the skyscraper of the telephone company is hidden by them. Our men lie in the trench, helpless. Nobody speaks; they ask themselves: "Didn't those bombs fall on our quarter — are my wife, my mother, my brother still alive at this moment?" They won't know until our company has had its full two weeks at the front and returns to the ruins of Madrid on leave. Irrespective of this I have not seen a single man whose determination was shaken by this terror. On the contrary, every

,ombardment makes their hate of fascism and their will to conquer
lame up.

"That is," says Fermin to me, "because we have known ever
,ince the start that there was no other choice but death or victory.
Every one of us is a volunteer and knows what he is fighting for.
We are a backward people as far as knowledge is concerned, but
they cannot deceive our hearts!"

That Fermin was right became evident several days ago when
the enemy threw another one of their propaganda packages behind
our lines with tens of thousands of throw-aways. Of course, nobody
thought of forbidding the men to pick up or read the leaflets. On the
contrary, officers and men ran like hares to get hold of one. Then —
did we laugh! It turned out to be quite a merry afternoon! I remember the illiterate Juan Antonio from the Fourth Platoon who had it
read to him three times over, by three different people, as though he
could not believe it. He looked at me questioningly: *"Que tonterias!"*
[what foolishness] "is it possible that they are that dumb?"

Indeed, the mixture of impudence, cynicism and fantastical lies
which not only fill these papers but are heard in the radio speeches
of Franco and that drunken Queipo de Llano, too, (we often hear
them over Radio-Burgos or Radio-Seville) is so obviously in direct
contradiction to the truth that even the simplest illiterate lad can
see through these lies because of his own practical knowledge.

Why is it that their propaganda is so clumsy?

It is because those who write this have never known the people
and themselves have come to believe in the picture of fear and
prejudice which they have painted. For them indeed "the people"
is synonymous with "stupid Red rabble" and their sickly imagination ascribes to them all the brutality which they fancied in their
sadistic dreams. How could they, who themselves have never suffered, be able to understand the everlasting tenderness and the
commiseration, born of sorrow, animating the soul of the people?
How could they, whose whole life has been dominated by the pursuit of money and power, be able to understand that the people
have other motives which drive them to battle than just greed?
How could they, who build their propaganda ministries on the sys-
tematic lies of big-business advertising, be able to understand the
primitive urge for candor which still exists in the unsophisticated

farmer? The propaganda leaflets of Franco would have worked very nicely with the bourgeois public of Holland; his mistake was that he distributed them among the working people.

Repeatedly the boys read one sentence to me, their voices shaking with indignation: "Spaniards, while you go hungry, your government pays most exorbitant salaries to foreign adventurers who with their weapons, wish to make your country into a Russian colony." Other boys scoffed: "Say, José, when we get to Madrid I guess you will treat, since we know now that you are a millionaire!"

Our boys know that Franco started this battle with Moorish mercenaries and with the foreign legion, in whose uniform many a German and Italian fascist hid himself.

Our boys know too that we stand at the same little wicket with them, officers and men alike, to get our monthly three hundred pesetas. Our boys know that we don't have any "recruiting stations" and that those who come here from other countries come voluntarily and often with the greatest trouble, without any promises and without any compensation over and above what is given to any Spanish laborer who joins the militia.

That accounts for the love, the admiration and the fondness that they bestow on us foreigners, and which often makes us ashamed of ourselves.

The Spanish people are a people of story tellers; even now, when we sit around the smoking wood fire in the evening, they are already weaving legends around the International Brigade. In the stories of the comrades, the fighters of the International Brigade become half-Gods, figures like the Cid or like the heroic knights who once routed the Moors from Spanish soil. The raconteur speaks with such respectful admiration of these heroes of the International Brigade that sometimes he seems to forget that he himself has been at the front for more than five months now. Still it has to be admitted that the boys of the International Brigade have indeed always given the example of bravery, sacrifice and discipline on the most threatened front.

A few days ago Domela said to me: "Haven't you noticed that we get larger rations at night lately?" "Yes," I answered, "the fare evidently is getting better." Domela shook his head, "If anything, the fare is getting worse, but they give us more than the others."

And that night we got a double portion of ham again. We went to
the captain to complain, but he just made a very mysterious face,
"Don't let that bother you, everything is okay!" We protested
energetically that it was not okay. It seemed that the militiamen
had met while we had been to the academy at night and had decided "that the two foreigners should have double rations, because
the rations that we get right now, since no hot food is getting
through, are less than adequate!" Need it be said that we henceforth refused to accept double rations at the expense of others,
much as we appreciated their good intentions?

I notice that this letter is getting excessively long. The militiamen look over my shoulders as I write. But still one more thing: in
cooperation with our political commissar, we have organized several
classes for illiterates, and even political recitals. Much to our disgust these evenings are all too often interrupted because of an aerial
attack or because of other unpleasant movements of the enemy.
But it is wonderful to see how much the militiamen care for all this;
they do everything they can to support us in every way. This afternoon I want to practise map reading again with the corporals and
sergeants. They should also know how to make a small sketch. It is
about time for me to start gathering the necessary material so I will
close this letter.

From Spanish Trenches

LAMBERT BEEKMANS is diametrically opposed to Last in every way. Their only thought in common is their desire to crush fascism. While Last is the writer and the philosopher, with years of political schooling, Beekmans' thoughts are simple, direct and unschooled. Probably these few letters are his very first attempts to place his thoughts on paper. Yet he expresses much feeling in his halting, laborious writing. Beekmans comes from the backward south of Holland. He earned his meagre living as a peddler. He went from door to door selling the necessities that a housewife buys. He depended on the contents of his little black suitcase for his daily bread.

The friendship which culminated in the writing of these letters is well worth mentioning. Going from door to door the peddler was invited in to share the none-too-luxurious board of a laborer and his large family. Later he visited these new friends whenever he passed through their city. From this man — a Catholic like himself, as well as an anti-fascist — he first learned about Spain and about fascism. One day, when passing through, he told his friend that he — since he had no one in the world — would like to go to Spain. He was advised not to go, since it might cost him his life. But he insisted and finally left for Spain toward the end of February 1937.

March 15, 1937

Friends:

I am for about a month in Spain now and we are still doing splendidly. I am here with a Flemish group, and we are doing splendidly. The fascists went on a great offensive on our front last week, but the result has been that he has been beaten back a few kilometers along the whole line, and that he has lost hundreds of dead; it has been a veritable butchery, behind every tree lay a corpse. Every day Spaniards come over to our side who have been forced to fight for Franco. We shall not rest until we have chased that fascist scum into the Mediterranean up to the last man. And how are things in Holland? If you could arrange to send us the papers, we would know what goes on in Holland, too. I hope that you will soon send me a few words, too, and I end with greetings from the Dutch and Flemish comrades,

LAMBERT BEEKMANS
3rd Comp. 11th Edgar André Brigade

62

Holland

April 2, 1937

Dear Friends:

I want to inform you that I have received your letter and also the newspaper. It made me happy to hear from my Dutch comrades here at the front. I did not know that the cost of the paper would be so high, and I am sure that if you have to pay for it yourself, that you will have to deprive your wife and children of things they need. But if it is the case that some of the comrades in Middelburg [a small, ancient city in the south of Holland] can spare some cigarettes and cigars we would greatly appreciate it here; here there is tobacco but it isn't fit to smoke. I am just two months here now. Of which one and a half at the front and I will try to give you a picture of conditions how things stand right now. We are at a turning point, first we had to defend tooth and nail, and now the tables have turned. Around Madrid they have been beaten back everywhere, for the town there is no immediate danger any more, then they have tried to surround Madrid by cutting the Valencia-Madrid road, they were all German fascists and Moors and foreign legionnaires, the result was that he lost thousands dead and was beaten back seven kilometers on top of that. But the finest success we booked on the Guadalajara front, it is on the big highway Madrid-Saragossa, there he made his last big attempt. Here it was Mussolini's servants, his blackshirts and his best troops from Abessinia, 40,000 in number had been collected here equipped with the most modern Italian weapons and tanks, but we, well supported by our brave Spanish comrades, were at our posts. Five long days the fight was heavy and bloody but on the sixth day came the reward, ours made a furious attack and we succeeded to break through their lines, then it was finished with them, it was not a retreat anymore but it became a wild flight twenty kilometers they were beaten back in two days, leaving behind sixteen cannons, sixty trucks, hundreds of machine guns, six wagonloads of ammunition blankets, tons of gasoline, shoes their field-kitchens were strewn all over. They had taken off their shoes to be able to run faster and still we made six hundred prisoners and the dead couldn't be counted. According to estimate they have lost material worth 16,000,000 pesetas in one day. So you see things go well here just now. I have to finish because I haven't time any more. Greet everybody in

63

From Spanish Trenches

Middelburg also your wife and children also from my Flemish comrades but especially from me,

COMRADE BEEKMANS

April 20, 1937, Guadalajara

Comrades:

You will be surprised to suddenly get so many letters from me but we are on rest so I have the time. I wrote about the smashing of Mussolini's servants on the Guadalajara front alas we have lost two Dutch and one Flemish comrade from our group. They fell like heroes at their post because they didn't want to retreat before the oncoming fascists who were ten times stronger than we. But we got our reward, March 20, the day that I became twenty six years old we advanced sixteen kilometers. Comrades we must weed out that barbarous fascism that can do nothing but murder women and children to the last man all over the world, long live the People's Front. Here we have the most beautiful example of solidarity, here they fight shoulder to shoulder, Hollanders, Belgians, French, Germans, English, anyhow all the nations of the world all together with one purpose, to beat fascism. Those poor fascists all run around with a beard a yard long and more they have sworn not to get shaved except in Madrid and now they cannot fight anymore because they are tripping all the time over their beards. Comrade, I close here with the best greetings to all but especially to you, your wife and children from me,

COMRADE BEEKMANS
No pasaran, nosotros pasaremos

64

CUBA

PABLO DE LA TORRIENTE BRAU, in his native Cuba, in 1930, joined a student demonstration against Machado. He was badly beaten up and spent many weeks in a hospital. In 1932 he had to leave Machado's Cuba. When he arrived in New York he sold ice cream in the streets. After the overthrow of Machado in 1933, he returned to Cuba. The most important Cuban newspaper, "Ahora," hired him as a reporter. Uncovering a hideous crime, involving the killing of three students by Havana's police chief Pedruza, cost him his job. Once more he was forced to join the exiles in New York. From here, when the war broke out, he went to Spain. He left his position as correspondent in Spain to fight in the Republican army. The letter which follows is his last one, for soon afterward he was killed in action.

Alcala de Henares, November 30, 1936

Here goes another letter. The cannon bark louder than ever. It seems that our batteries have been increased considerably and that they have orders to do a little destructive work. There is plenty of booming from the other side as well. I have just arrived from Pozuelo de Alarcon, a tiny town with twisted and climbing streets and white houses with blue mosaic bases jutting from their thick brick walls. Until last night the battalion was there, and now when I managed to rejoin it they have transferred us to Alcala de Henares, the city where Cervantes was born. At this rate I will soon have covered half of Spain.

The other day an insolent squadron of fifteen Italian tri-motors, accompanied by pursuit planes, flew over Madrid early in the day and unloaded in a brutal, pitiless manner. These dogs are murdering more women and children in Madrid than men on the front. In the crowded workers' neighborhood, Quatro Caminos, the bombs smashed streetcars full of people. It was an especially hard day at several points along the Madrid front. The Frenchman's Bridge, where the enemy started a desperate attack, had to be blown up. Their tactic hasn't changed, and as a matter of fact, it cannot very

65

well be changed. No other road is open to them but to capture Madrid, and they won't be able to do that.

Despite the deficiencies of our infant military apparatus, despite a harmful inactivity on other fronts at a moment when there should be greater pressure from our forces, they won't enter. Moreover they may soon have to flee. Our aviation is wrecking their bases and their planes on a large scale. But they always restore these; their planes fly directly from Germany and Italy, traveling over France by night. If France did as much as the fascists of Europe, the war would soon be over. The indebtedness of the Spanish fascists to Germany and Italy is growing alarmingly. It may become so huge that there will be no solution but an international war. How the artillery is thundering! It's worth listening to, if only once in a lifetime. It's like a tempest of thunder and lightning in the mountains of Oriente in Cuba. Their aviation, which has shown itself to be inferior to ours in close fighting, does not tire of acts of vandalism which defy description. Last night, after a thrilling beating which they had received during the afternoon from our machines, their planes appeared and threw incendiary bombs on the city. In the blackness of the night, there arose over the horizon, out towards the Casa de Campo, the glare of the fire they had caused. A hospital was also bombarded. Such are the methods of their desperation. Every time I feel their cannon closer to Madrid I fancy ours closer to Seville and Burgos. I suppose that the international press has mentioned something about their most recent bestiality. They dropped a box by parachute over Madrid containing the horribly cut-up body of one of our aviators who had fallen behind their lines. Not even the cannibal tribes would do this — they are not exhibitionists of barbarism. On our side, General Miaja, head of the Defense Junta, has just issued an order that the lives of all fascist aviators who fall over Madrid be respected.

At dawn yesterday an intense shelling took place. In the neighborhood of Abascal and Quevedo Streets, the smoke and the crashes of falling buildings filled the air. Families evacuated their homes, weeping, dragging their children along and leaving the dead behind. But not far from the spot, hundreds of men were engaged in military drill, preparing to leave for the front. I went to the nearby temporary headquarters of the International Red Aid which had been forced out of its old home by the shelling of the Montana barracks. I went to see how things were getting along there and incidentally to see whether there was any news from you. (By the way, now that I am "authority" around here, when you write to me, do so adding the words "Commissario de Guerra.") At the International Red Aid, there were, as always, hundreds of women and children refugees who had fled from the shelling, and many waiting around, resting on mountains of clothing, for a chance to be sent to Barcelona and Valencia. The kids leave here in large buses, singing, waving their little red flags. It doesn't occur to one that many of them are or will be orphans. It doesn't occur to one because the revolution is mother to all; she will give birth with more blood and pain than any mother, to a new people. I think with deep joy of what this country will be like afterwards. It excites me. Spain will be marvellous. The harder and more cruel the war, the greater and more quickly will all of that come about. Yesterday, by the way, I felt another of war's emotions: that of being in Madrid as just another militiaman. The feeling of "coming to Madrid" to forget all, to think not even of myself, as come the men from the front who look forward to the chance of being here a few hours, of seeing the sparkling eyes of the women and drinking in the taverns among care-free friends. A bit of ruddy wine which glows like the lanterns in the red-light district, and mugs of beer, brown and foamy, like the German sweethearts of some of the members of the International Brigade. And then we went, a group of comrades, to the Laurel Inn. Having drunk marquis' wine in quantities, we ate varied dishes, rare things which we had not seen for three months. There was old wine. There were women with shining, black hair and white smiles, mysterious eyes like ancient stones, and soft white hands. But who thinks of women now? I tell you, though, living is a beautiful thing. And the wine of Spain enlivens one's fancy without making you drunk. At least it doesn't make me drunk.

From there I went to see a bit of destruction and a bit of another red object — blood. Near the Plaza de España there was a dead horse. Some children, with the carelessness of a people playing with life and death, with the same detachment as if it were gambling in the lottery, were talking about the war. One said, "You have to watch out. We were there and all of a sudden, ssshiii! . . .

67

Lucky we threw ourselves on the ground." I kept walking along, and suddenly it was I who had to drop to the ground. How quickly I've learned to judge distance and danger by sound. Bits of rock and shell sprayed against a wall I was passing. That neighborhood has been severely punished, and still there are those — heroes or imbeciles or needy ones — who inhabit it. It seems as if the clamor of our batteries protects them. I passed a house half-smashed by an air bomb, which had also torn a small tree nearby from its roots. Then I ran into Francisco Sanchez, a comrade from La Tribuna, the People's Theatre. With some satisfaction he told me, "Two of our fellows have died on the front and two have been wounded." He gave me news about the Frenchmen's Bridge, where the fighting by that time had eased somewhat. It was already very late and I had to return because it was already time for "Campesino" [the "Peasant," commander of Pablo's battalion] to be back at our headquarters. At that time of day, the sound of the machine guns gets to be like that of a thick soup boiling and bubbling in some immense cauldron.

One doesn't feel in war. Last night I was returning with "Campesino" in the car and I held the diary of a deserter, just executed. We joked, in the most natural manner, about how his corpse would be cold under the inclement night and the frozen interminable drizzle.

I was once a man with feelings and I will become one again. The other night, while a problem was being debated, Lopez, Pepe Galan's aide, turned on the car's radio. We were in the middle of a silent battlefield, near the enemy. They were playing one of the most sensitive Chopin ballades, which I had often heard in quite another setting — the concert hall. While I strained to hear sounds of the enemy nearby, I remembered with a certain measure of nostalgia the time when music had other horizons for me than the hymn of revolution, inharmoniously intoned by companies in march — raucous, intense.

As I thought of other times while the Chopin ballade played, Lopez said to me: "You like this, don't you?" I remember his words, because, the following night, along the same road, he disappeared, probably forever. Probably one of their surprise detachments, in a swift action, captured him together with his traveling companions.

He was a jolly fellow, extremely clever. Everyone liked him, but now he is forgotten, at least until the war is over. It's three days now since he was lost. During this time I have been simultaneously in and out of Madrid. "Campesino" has received instructions to re-organize his battalion, decimated by the fighting at Pozuelo and Aravaca, and to create an additional one as well. Alcala de Henares is to serve as his organizing center. We have our headquarters in the convent of Las Claras. Miguel de Cervantes Saavedro was born and lived in Alcala de Henares. I have not had the time to visit his home. From our auto, I have seen that it is an ancient town with that simple dignity typical of Castile. Large buildings of old brick; elegant church towers and convents; a peaceful silence in the streets. It also has its plaza for band concerts, its original fiestas, and numerous artistic and historical treasures. They say, too, that its almonds are famous. And I can't tell you anything more of Alcala de Henares. Someday I'll know it better.

Today has begun badly for me. They have told me that Candon, the other Cuban commandant, has died. How happy he was to tell me the other day: "I'm going to lead the attack." Let's hope it is not true. He wanted me to go with him. As to the general atmosphere, it seems unchanged. The defense Junta has turned out to be a very efficient organism for the time and circumstances in which it was created. There's more unity and strictness in things. The enemy's so-called "Fifth Column" [fascists who remained hidden in Madrid and conducted night raids] has seen its possibilities for action shrink because of the measures taken, and the popular morale is as high as ever. On the whole, the press has recently maintained the vibrant tone which the moment demands. The newspapers have stopped their campaign against the transfer of the government to Valencia. It should be said that this measure was wholly correct and should even have been taken at an earlier date. Of course, there were individuals who, on their own, took the occasion to "transfer" themselves personally. But no one is to blame for that, and already each organization has taken appropriate measures against this. Many will never be able to return to Madrid, unless as cowards they have lost all sense of shame, something which is possible after all. But then again, we have the case of Don Ramon Menandez Pidal, who was given permission by the Ministry of

From Spanish Trenches

Public Instruction to leave for Cuba for a lecture series a month ago, and who has refused to leave Madrid while the present situation persists. He is a man of learning, a cordial and simple person to whom the crashing of shells can hardly be agreeable, but here he remains with us. Well, I leave off here. I will write you from the land of Cervantes.

GERMAN EMIGRÉS

ALFRED KANTOROWICZ kept a diary during his first few months in Spain. These notes, parts of which appear now for the first time, were not written for publication. They are notes stored away for future reference by an author who knows that a quick succession of important occurrences tends to fade in the mind. They were sent on urgent request for experiences of Germans in Spain. Kantorowicz is secretary of the International Writers' Congress. He is also on the executive board of the German Writers' Union in Paris.

December 12, 1936

For three long days Madrid had been hidden in a fog so thick that at times you could not see two yards in front of you. Quiet on all fronts.

Early yesterday the fog lifted, and I went to Fifth Regiment Headquarters to get Kurt. We drove off to the front.

I asked why this section of the army which by now comprised some tens of thousands of men, formed into numerous brigades, should merely be called: The Fifth Regiment. "Well," he explained, "the four regiments garrisoned in Madrid when the revolt started, joined Franco. Out went the call for a new regiment — the Fifth. Within a few days thousands had volunteered and were ready for combat. And by now the Fifth numbers over 60,000 men. Its name, however, no longer signified an army unit, but Madrid's volunteers as a whole. Carlos, political commissar, whose acquaintance I made yesterday, has made a name for himself as their organizer; as their outstanding army leader they named Lister, a peasant's son.

In an outlying workers' section, on the road to Fuencarral, a woman lay in our path. We stopped short. She was dead. Bystanders told our driver she had been shot in the back in the early morning hours.

"Who shot her?"

"The Fifth Column." A bullet through her lung, another through the neck. Her face was turned to the ground. She was a well known Socialist functionary, they told us. They were waiting for the

death-wagon to come and take the corpse. All this we were
told in the most matter of fact tones. The sight of death has become part of any day's casual occurrences and no longer creates
any sensation.

The "Fifth Column," Kurt explains as we drive on again, is a
strong, active fascist band within Republican territory: Regular
Army Officers, *falangistas*, hired thugs, spies, saboteurs, assassins,
who, from within, attempt to assist the four Franco columns advancing on Madrid. After their first brash efforts, they have become
more wary. Yet driving back from the front nights, one does well to
have a gun handy.

At every crossroad we are challenged. Kurt answers, "International Brigade." A magic word — an Open Sesame. There is a
warm feeling for these battalions of anti-fascists: French, Italian,
German, Polish, Hungarian, Jugoslav, Belgian, Czech, English,
American. To be part of them gives one a glow of pride and happiness. To be able to say, "I belong to the Eleventh Brigade — The
International," is a better recommendation than distinction of rank
or worldly fame. As I sense this, I am impatient to get into uniform
and "belong." Already, today, I have received my baptism of fire
— plenty of it. This gives me a little right to say "I belong."

Nine-thirty found us passing through Fuencarral. We made a
brief stop at a German battery and drove on to headquarters in L.
A gorgeous day, remarkably clear for miles around. Before us the
snow-covered Guadarramas, shining in the sun. All is quiet, peaceful. A peace which any one of us, ready to fight through until victory is ours, would gladly see realized soon.

At headquarters we are told the situation is serious. Our battalions have been pushed back in several places. But reinforcements
are expected momentarily. Our line has only to hold a few hours
more and we will settle accounts. For that evening a counter-attack
has been planned. With a decisive battle being fought, how can
these men, one wonders, go on with their paper work? They urge us
to go to the battalions which are the thick of it.

Kurt arranges with the headquarters commander to leave with
him within the hour to carry orders to the battalion. I ask to go
along. Kurt hesitates. Is a civilian's life more valuable than the life
of a man in uniform, I ask. He puts the matter up to Hans. It takes

ne a while to get to Hans, but he consents. I get myself a gun, a
artridge belt, and wait. Our departure is delayed. In the afternoon
s we are lolling in front of headquarters three bombers appear.
hey are Junkers, well known to the boys by now. They excite
ore curiosity than fear. Headquarters turns out to take a good
ok at them. They head right toward us, true, they are high enough
p — some 6000 feet, I should think. Suddenly they let loose.
oom — only fifty yards off, in the vegetable garden; zoom — zoom
— zoom — zoom in the flower garden. The cries of a child, as a
ttle ten year old girl comes running across the field, with blood on
er face. Nothing much, a shrapnel splinter scraped her. We take
he child into the house. Outside some one yells, "They're turning
ack!" The Junkers, of course. And now on the other side of head-
uarters the same business over again: zoom — zoom — zoom —
oom. Thirty yards off, fifty, now only twenty. The house shakes.
Will they hit? They mean to keep at it all day, it seems. We all
le into a little bit of a room now. Somebody hurrying in anxiously
lams the door behind him. A very young militiaman beside me
lumps in a heap. An officer, nervous and pale, yells: "It's only the
oor, man," and opening it he slams it to again amidst the thud and
hunder of the bombs, causing the whole structure to vibrate. The
oung militiaman breaks into tears.

Three o'clock and at last we can be on our way. We must first go
o the Spanish reserve battalions. A few kilometers brings us within
ange of the firing. The road we should take is under heavy fire.
We detour.

In the World War I had never had the experience of being under
hell fire while riding in a car. I sit here at the mercy of chance,
vith no way of defending myself. Some fifty yards behind us — the
pot where we were only a second or two ago — a shell explodes. I
egin to get jittery. Of course, I keep this from the others. But I
each a definite conclusion: I am far indeed from being that reck-
ess, laughing boy of eighteen, who, in the attack on Combles, was
lways out there ahead of his company, calling back cheerily to his
ommanding officer, "This beats your drilling all hollow!" The
abandon with which I would brave the heaviest barrage — my
fear becoming a thrill — was merely lack of imagination. I was
cockeyed to believe it was courage. Have I really got courage?

73

From Spanish Trenches

The test has still to be made when I learn to look danger, as danger
straight in the eye and know fear for what it is. Having ironed out
my thoughts on that score, I regain that peace of mind which is so
necessary for the job in hand.

We come to the spot where we have to get out and walk. Across
the fields we scurry, all three of us. We make our way across a small
stream with the water up to our belts. Funny outfit I was wearing.
My old black tuxedo, made to order sixteen years ago and con-
verted some seasons back into a business suit; my topcoat, bought
in Capri, nearly as old and perhaps even more incongruous; my
Paris-made oxfords and silk socks. All taken in conjunction with
my gun and cartridge-belt and myself wading waist-high through
the ice-cold current must have made a comical sight for anybody to
see.

We convey a message to a Spanish battalion in the first line of
reserves to move up to the front lines. That is our entire mission,
then back to the car by wading the brook again. Now, however,
we must go ahead quickly to the German battalions. It is half-past
four and night will fall in less than an hour. Probably the counter
attack has already started.

Our artillery has been firing over our heads without a moment's
let-up. We can see the shells burst perhaps two miles ahead. Our
front lines must therefore be no further than a mile and a half away.
Spanish militiamen stopped our car to ask directions and to get a
lift to the front for some of their number.

While we are palavering, planes come speeding in our direction —
we count nine of them. They drop bombs on the road before us.
They are our own planes, assisting in the counter attack, we say.
They dive low and clip away at the lines with machine gun fire.
Now they turn and come right at the forty of us. One man yells,
"Fascists!" Instantly we scatter for cover. Some twenty yards
further on is a ditch which might afford some minimum of protection. As I throw myself into it, the planes are over our heads, thirty
yards from the ground at the most. We recognize them and they us.
They are our own men. Had they been fascists not one of us would
have lived to tell the tale. Never as in those brief moments have I
so utterly had the sense of helplessness in the face of odds: unarmed,
exposed, there I was in a ditch that gave no real protection. I was

74

prepared neither physically nor psychologically to cope with flying
war machines that grimly droned overhead with a speed of 400
kilometers.

We are together again, the Spanish comrades and ourselves.
Bullets whiz and fragments of bursting grenades hiss by us. Finally,
we come to a trench or rather the markings of an intended trench,
behind the low walls of which are two Spanish companies, the men
stripped bare to the waist. Kurt and the headquarters officer identify themselves. And there, under fire, we bring our heads together
in earnest parley.

Madrid, December 24, 1936

The battalions are resting but ready for action at a moment's
notice, for on the other side the recent savage attacks have stopped
suspiciously. Our Spanish battalions, having relieved the Thaelmann and André battalions, had succeeded this morning in taking
several kilometers of territory without firing a shot, territory which
had cost many a sacrifice already. What does it mean? Demoraliza-
tion, weakness, mutiny or trickery? Mutiny, perhaps, as our troops
find the bodies of a good many fascist officers.

We also see the bodies of comrades from the Thaelmann battalion, fifteen from the storm troop — twelve Germans, three
Englishmen — who alone held three fascist companies at bay,
fighting till they had fired their last shot and then fighting on again
with bayonet, gun butt and knife. They might have sought safety,
or they were ordered to retreat, but they sent back word that their
retreat might result in the Edgar André battalion being cut off.
So they stood their ground and halted the decisive push in the
Boadilla woods. At least 200 fascists bled to death in front of that
human wall. They held their position and they fell, man after man;
twelve German and three English soldiers of freedom fell in hand-
to-hand combat. We shall bury them after tomorrow in the Fuencarral cemetery.

December 25, 1936

Hans pointed out today how twenty years ago he, a German
officer, and Dumont, a French officer, were lying opposite each

other at "Dead Man." They discovered this while talking together
"Now," Hans said, "Germans and Frenchmen are fighting side by
side against a common enemy, international fascism. And side by
side we will defeat that common enemy." A French comrade added
"That's more to the purpose, hein?" and we all joined in a loud
laugh of good cheer, to think how these few weeks had so tried our
comradeship in arms and understanding, for all our individual
character as Germans and Frenchmen, that we were welded to
gether in a unity of purpose.

January 3, 1937

My brief talk in the theatre was patterned after the New Year
appeal to the brigades which I had written a few days before
Reading it through again for the occasion, I was a little abashed by
the optimism of this call which I had written under the impression
that the fascists were definitely licked when their great offensive
failed. The quiet on all fronts was too profound. Hitler and Musso
lini won't admit defeat so quickly. It will be a bloody year. And
while our slogan "Nosotros Pasaremos" of 1937 should replace the
"No Pasaran" of 1936, this will probably take quite some time to
realize.

January 5, 1937

We're living through some pretty tough days. The united fascis
forces have been attacking with fury, and have captured places
Majadahonda is in their hands, and possibly, by now, Las Rosas
which commands the main road to the Escorial. And its driving
force has not yet been spent. We can expect other fierce attacks in
the next few days. The city is under fire. Air raids every few hours
German and Italian tanks, German and Italian flyers, German and
Italian artillery, German and Italian officers: these are the forces
engaged in this drive. That is no longer civil war. It is war between
the fascist states on the one side and the Spanish people on the
other. London can go on investigating with its committees for
years, falsifying the facts which are plain as your boots, refusing to
see what the whole world sees, turning a deaf ear to what the whole

world hears: that there is a war on between the people of Spain, and Germany and Italy, who are using a pack of Spanish traitors and scoundrels for their purpose.

A tough day: for me too. Early this morning I heard from Nicoletti that Ralph Fox was killed. He was political commissar of the British company. I had always hoped to meet him again. I regarded him highly, as writer, as organizer and as comrade. He had been the firm and active nucleus of the British revolutionary writers' movement. Every time I met and worked with him I was confirmed in my impression of him as an example: able, yet unassuming and modest; but firm in matters of principle; his forthrightness and his complete lack of vanity. A man of good common sense and sound understanding. A writer with great abilities which had not yet fully matured. Although he was my junior by a year or two (born in 1900 or 1901, I think) and showed toward me a sincere spirit of comradeship at all times, I had the respect for him right from the beginning that would have been more properly the due of an older man. He never vaunted himself or his accomplishments. He hardly ever spoke about himself. Here he lived, fought and died as a company commander. Such few bulletins as mentioned him spoke of his rare courage and comradeship. His death is a great loss to anti-fascist literature, yes, to the anti-fascist movement.

I was instructed to go to the Telefónica and break the news to Fox's friends in London and Paris. I got some material together and did not get away until about noon. When we got to the Plaza Tetuán we were showered with bombs. Straight above were twenty-three Junkers and Capronis. Women snatched up their children and fled. Now it hit on the right by the subway entrance. On, on, it is crazy to stop here, I yelled to the driver, and dodging through the running, screaming people he got around the corner to the Telefónica. But the telephone building was the bombers' target. We tore straight through the bombardment; right, left, before us and behind us houses cracked and tumbled amid an infernal din. We skirted immense holes in the ground that hadn't been there a minute ago. The raid had taken a toll of over 300 lives according to figures obtainable late this afternoon. On their return flight, after dropping their bombs in the heart of town, these flyers directed their machine gun fire at women and children in the suburbs. That is "Fascism"! When did the world ever see the like? How feeble, how meaningless are the words with which one might attempt to describe it. Italian and German airmen dropping to within 200 feet of the earth in order to mow down rows of women and children who have been standing in line to get some food. That is "Fascism"! The bodies of women and children laid out in rows on the streets of Madrid; such is the picture by which history will identify this human scourge throughout the world. How grateful must we be who are there, privileged to atone for this disgrace to our people with our work and with the lives of the best among us.

In the telephone building we ran into the crowd of people who were rushing down the stairs to find refuge in the cellar, much too late, since the flyers had passed by already. The telefónica had not been hit; they seldom hit their mark. I forced my way through. Upstairs the imperturbable Spanish telephone operator was at his post. Still out of breath, I asked him to get me Paris. In half a minute he had made the connection. Friedel was at the other end. I knew she would be in the office today and I was terribly glad to have the chance to speak to her. I thought it would take half an hour to get the connection, during which time I planned to put my thoughts together and set down the most important questions in writing, hoping that the many things I wanted to tell her would not suddenly make me tongue-tied and allow banalities to take the place of things which are so important. I know from experience what it means after weeks of absence to hear a wife's voice again and to have only two minutes in which to pour out one's heart. One manages to say just nothing.

I knew all this but the connection was made so quickly that I was in exactly the predicament I had hoped to avoid. I still had the roar of the bombs, the shrieks of the victims in my ears, and I had not yet caught my breath — and I already heard my wife's voice from the Paris office.

"Hello," I said, "how are you?" I had to repeat that, the connection was bad. "Thanks, I'm all right, quite all right . . . I'm feeling fine . . . No, no, everything's all right over here . . . Oh, the air raids? They're not like you think. No, you get used to them . . . Have you found anybody to sublease the apartment?" Then fifteen seconds silence while I fumble over what to say. I

ouldn't think of anything and neither could Friedel, it seemed.
'he call had taken her by surprise. Then we began asking after
eople: Kurt and Gustav, Mieke and Jeanne, and finally I asked
er to have M. come to the phone. And I made my report to him.
I did not want to tell her outright Fox had died as she had known
im and thought a lot of him.) After I laid down the receiver I
emembered all the things I had wanted to tell her.

Toward evening the difficulty of the situation became evident.
Dumont of the "Commune de Paris" battalion, was wounded. His
olitical commissar reported: the battalion had had to meet the
runt of the attack. Additional information was brought from head-
uarters by Kurt. He had a young Austrian along, wounded last
November, who had rejoined the André battalion only day before
esterday, who got it for the second time today: shot through the
houlder. We took him to the hospital where the victims of the
morning's air raids had just been operated on and bandaged; and
lready those wounded in the battle, who could be moved, were
eing brought in on stretchers. They slumped on the benches, or
emained lying on the stretchers. Blood oozed through the flimsy
andages and dripped over their uniforms and onto the floor. The
loctors stuck to their jobs like machines, never even looking up.
The smell of iodine and blood was all over the place. One man
omited. Another groaned to himself, softly. A third would let out
 shriek ever so often. War is hell, more terrible in the city here
han out there in the trenches.

January 8, 1937

This evening Hans, brigade chief; Richard, commander of the
Thaelmann battalion; Wilhelm, commander of the Edgar André,
he man taking the place of Dumont, whose wounds fortunately
re not serious, came over to see Nicoletti. There came too the
olitical commissars of the battalions: Artur from the Thaelmann,
Paul from the André, and Ribière from the Commune de Paris.
But what a condition they came in! Richard, the man of iron, the
oremost battalion commander, the best of friends and comrades —
 could almost cry to think of it and wouldn't be ashamed if I did —
Richard was pale as wax, with quivering hands, his face sunken,

79

his features moving convulsively. I had to turn away. Hans, alway
serene and cheerful, who keeps his nerve and his good humor unde
the most trying circumstances, had dark rings under his eyes an
looked worried and all done in. Ribière, the "playboy," always gay
always up to tricks, brave as they come, the finest of comrade
Ribière threw himself into a chair, dropped his head in his hand
and cried as if his heart would break. Even Nicoletti had to mak
an effort to keep from crying. Nobody spoke. Nobody dared as
where is this fellow or that one.

Then Hans spoke up: even though the battle had meant th
sacrifice of our best men, the fascist drive had been stopped, brough
to a definite halt with only a few kilometers in their favor. One
more Madrid is saved. They didn't pass and they shan't pass.

January 9, 1937

The brigade will come back for a rest, for replacements and re
organization. Last night was the hardest of any that I experience
in Madrid. Do the fascists seek vengeance or do they really suppos
that they can obtain that which they failed to win in open comba
by striking terror into the city?

While we were eating in the canteen of the Fifth Regiment, th
shots fell about us, a hundred yards off, two hundred yards, fift
yards. The building rattled, windows crashed, women screame
and rushed to the door, even men got to their feet — for no goo
reason, for either the shot struck on the instant or they had passe
by already.

We sat down again. I looked round at the faces. The men wer
trying to smile, a little ashamed of themselves. All were pale, eve
those who had survived a hundred air raids. Here in a house insid
the city, it is not the same as out there where there are only mer
We decided these were the "fat ones," probably the 120-kilo bomb
Some left to see where they had struck.

Within half an hour the planes were back, this time with in
cendiary bombs. Fires started in all directions. It is remarkabl
that when morning comes the widespread damage will hardly b
noticed: the fires will have been put out, the debris cleared, th
holes in the pavement patched. It is precisely in these things tha

e morale of the Madrileños shows up best, in the matter of fact-
ss with which such evidently necessary jobs are dispatched.
ladrid takes these disasters of the past several months as if they
ere little street accidents which get straightened out simply as
art of the day's work. Fires are extinguished, holes in the ground
lled up, debris removed, and by morning Madrid wakes up and
nds the city getting along pretty much "as usual." One has to
ok close to notice that a building here and another there has dis-
ppeared during the night, and that the streets display so many new
elltale patches of asphalt.

Tonight they came almost at half-hour intervals, dropping in-
endiary bombs, heavy bombs, medium-sized bombs; at half past
ine, at ten, eleven, half past eleven, and so on. About eleven the
rtillery got going. At midnight fierce fighting was in progress
t Porte Moncloa about three kilometers from our place, but it
ounded as though there was shooting in the next block. After a
hile, no mistake about it, there was fighting around the corner,
ith rifles and machine guns. Carlos got his men together, we took
ur weapons, too. "Fifth Column?" Or did the fascists hordes break
hrough? After all it is only a matter of two or three kilometers
rom the front to the heart of the city. Of course, it was only nerv-
usness. Down the street some one had started shooting and in the
eneral high-strung atmosphere amid bombing attacks, thundering
rtillery, fighting at Porte Moncloa, an imaginary battle had broken
ut right in the street. The fascists had unquestionably given the
ignal, for this sort of thing had been happening too systematically.
Through some unlighted window a machine gun salvo would pour
nto the street and the fracas would begin. There are foreign con-
ulates known to house whole companies of organized fascists.

. . . Half past two in the afternoon. They are here again. On the
street people start to run. Quite a few, however, take their time,
uriously watching to see where the planes will drop their bombs.
The spirit here is almost miraculous. Day by day the fascists hurtle
heir bombs on the masses of people, aiming their machine guns at
groups of women and children. Yet no sooner is another day's
orror done, than the smiling girls are back on the streets, the
vomen singing as they hang out the wash on the roofs, children
playing in the streets, old women sitting on benches in the sun; while

81

the streetcars, full-up, with a complete panoply of flags, skid by th
scenes of the latest bombings. Hardly have the dead and wounde
been removed than the queue of women reforms at the food shop
if they had bothered to break their line while the raid was on.

The city freezes, for there is no coal. The city goes hungry, fo
food is scarce. The city does without almost everything, and live
in constant danger. Yet I have still to hear any grumbling or t
observe anything resembling panic. If ever a people deserved th
adjective heroic they are the people of Madrid, and not just th
men, much more so, perhaps more than any of them, the women
But for the calm and uncomplaining attitude of the Madrileña
but for their sweeping will to resist, Madrid could never have hel
out.

January 10, 1937

Last evening Walter came. He is chief of Company One of th
Thaelmann battalion. He brought me the papers of a Nazi flye
Sergeant Kneiding of the Immelmann pursuit squadron, who ha
been brought down. Our Walter, who had only recently come fro
the hospital, was nevertheless the first one to reach the fallen ma
chine. After one look at the pilot, who was dead, he exclaimed
"Kneiding!" He had known him well. Together they had serve
in the same air battalion, Walter as sergeant-major and Kneidin
a sergeant under him. Kneiding was dead and Walter the first t
reach him. Here is the material for a story which cannot be use
because as fiction it would sound unreal. Walter brought me th
man's papers, letters and pictures of his sweetheart — all of whic
I sent along this morning.

*GEORGE FELIX has been an exile from his native Germany sinc
1933. The letter which follows is to a friend in Paris.*

Dear Friend:

You know, of course, that women are not admitted to activ
service on the front. Still there are cases where sisters fight wit

eir brothers and wives with their husbands. In that respect the
panish women have splendid examples. I guess you still have their
reatest champion on the picture of the striking Asturian moun-
aineers which hangs on the wall in your room. La Pasionaria, that
, the ideal for these fighting anti-fascist women! I want to paint
ou some of these brave girls and women, who I met in the last
w weeks:

In the village about which I wrote you in my last letter, there was
n old lady, who had a little candy store and who also served coffee,
hich she prepared herself. A bunch of us would often stop by there.
he first time we were there, the old woman told us that her only
on had fallen on the Madrid front and that she was left behind now
vith her two daughters. The tears streamed down her face when she
old us that all her life she had saved for him, and that now, when
he was old while he had reached the best years of his youth, he had
o fall in the battle against the fascists. And so his death had become
he grave of all her hopes. Then she called both of her daughters,
 fourteen year old child and a girl of eighteen, and had us under-
tand that they thought just like their fallen brother, and wanted
o replace him in her heart. Every time we came to the old mother,
he called her older daughter to have her serve us. In Spain that is
 big honor; in the villages young girls do not serve in public es-
ablishments. Fourteen days after we had left the village I passed
hrough once more on a transport, and we did not neglect to pay a
visit to the old woman. She wept with joy when she saw us and told
us we were her sons, we belonged to the family and asked us if we
had beaten the fascists already.

For eight days we lay in a village a few kilometers behind the
front, along with us were several companies of Spaniards. A column
of anarchists was quartered across the way from us. Two girls belonged with their outfit, dressed and armed like their male companions. From one of the girls I learned the motive of her enlistment in the Battalion: she is from X. Her parents are still there and
she hasn't heard a word from any of her relatives since the military
putsch. She doesn't know whether they're still alive or whether they
have been shot by the fascists long ago. It so happens that the town
has been in the hands of the fascists since the first days of the putsch
and is beleaguered by us.

From Spanish Trenches

Women are not admitted into the battalion unless there is som
specific reason. But in this case her request was granted withou
hesitation. She would have been despised if she had acted otherwis

Then we came to a large place. The civil population had bee
partly cleared out, because it was often subjected to aerial attack
by the enemy. While we were there, the enemy tried to bombar
the village three times. In such cases the population went into hid
ing, mostly just out into the open. At the city-limits we met thre
women with their small children; they held them by the hand c
carried them in their arms. We started a conversation with th
women, to give them courage. Thereupon the young mothers ex
plained to us that they only went to bring their children to a saf
place and that an older woman, the grandmother, would stay wit
the youngsters. The women went back to the village to continu
with their work. (Washing soldiers' clothes and helping with cook
ing and first-aid work.) On such days the children stayed out in th
open all day long under the supervision of some of the older womer
while those women who were able continued their work regardles
of plane alarms. With a most surprising calm, these women brough
their loved ones to safety so that they might do the work that th
civil war had allotted to them.

On the twenty-sixth at six o'clock in the morning we started ou
attack on Y. Our company gave excellent account of itself and a
eleven o'clock we were in possession of all the positions that we had
taken and we were on the last incline before the town. At our righ
a Spanish Battalion covered our flank. The Spaniards are by natur
an extremely brave people. Our closed and fast advance had awak
ened an enthusiasm in them that pushed them forward. The
wanted to advance together with us. Together with us they oc
cupied the last positions and passed them to get at the town. The
were commanded by a young militia officer whose bride fought sid
to side with him. She was armed with a revolver and always in th
first lines. She was dressed in a sportskirt and a pullover with a
rolled collar, she wore high boots and ran around very straigh
under the fire so that it looked as though she were on an equestria
path instead of in the front line of the firing. A glorious picture o
beauty, the way she stood at her post bravely and unconcernedly
The civil war knows no limits. The last vestiges of decency, ever

84

ose of the remotest human race, are trampled underfoot. There
no protection, either during the fighting or during "rest" i.e.,
hen there doesn't happen to be any fighting going on, for the
ospital personnel. In order to bring in one badly wounded comrade,
hree unarmed stretcher bearers had to lose their lives. Notwith-
tanding their red-cross sleeveband they are simply shot down by
he fascists. There is no quarter given in Spain. I already informed
ou in my last letter, that Jan had fallen; it was in this battle that
e was so badly maimed. About a half an hour later he died from
is wounds. We carried him to the field hospital, which was about
wo hundred yards behind the line. In an empty sheepstall they
ad installed a first-aid station; a Spanish physician was in charge,
t his side was his wife who received the wounded. When for about
ight or ten hours troops are storming enemy positions, when there
s shooting from rifles, machine guns and tanks, you can just about
magine what goes on in a first-aid station in the front line. And, in
he midst of the groaning wounded, and the dead who were laid out,
he wife of the physician accomplished her work with a calm that
vorked on everybody like magic. When, excited and all out of
oreath, we carried in the mortally wounded Jan, she took his hand
almly and said: "Your friend is dying, there is nothing you can do
or him."

I will never be able to fulfill my duty in the firing line with such
omplete preparedness, nor be able to accept death like this brave
woman —

It becomes possible to understand how great these Spanish women
are only when one considers that not until now has the Spanish
woman been awakened to political life and been freed from centuries
of backwardness. This exclusion of the Spanish woman in the old
Spain is best expressed in the rigid interpretation of customs and
morals, which exclude the Spanish girl from all activity outside of
the family circle. This even extends to the most progressive part of
the youth, into which the Socialist and Communist youth are
organized as well as the militia formations. After the parade, after
the demonstration and after the political group gathering or the
open meeting the young woman does not go home without her
mother, nor does she go out walking with her friend unaccompanied.

I have never before seen such rigid isolation or even suspected its

existence. In the country this incredible condition is even more pre
historic. There the girl is nothing but a regular "family prisoner"
and even in clear daylight she never goes into the street alone, a
the very least she is accompanied by a girl friend.

↔

WILI is a young German fighting in the International Brigade.

December 5, 1936

Dear friends:

Mola wanted to be in Madrid by November 6. Two weeks later
he hadn't come yet. We waited for him and all we got was six car
full of fascist newspapermen who took their Mola seriously and ex
pected to be in on his triumphal march into the city. The reception
they got was not exactly a friendly one and they are anxiously
looking forward to the time when they can go to work again. Which
should be along about doomsday. And now Mola has cracked another, announcing he will be here by Christmas. Just a little tip to
the kiddies so they should prepare for Black Peter. [In Germany
Santa Claus is always accompanied by a black servant, Peter, who
puts bad children into the bag that held the presents for the good
children.]

Our army is organized differently now. Before you could find
formations made up of various parties along any section of the
front, each with its own command whose orders were final. Add the
modern weapons which will be coming along and you can see that
we will be showing the fascists a new sort of resistance. And add the
heightened morale and the increased confidence. What a different
feeling it is when the fascists launch a tank attack to see our own
tanks creeping up from back of our lines, to hear the lively backtalk
of our MG's and our revolving cannon. I want to tell you a story
about this. We boys were with our company right up in the front
sector occupied by the International Brigade. Under cover of a
heavy fog, we had entrenched ourselves on a low hill. Before us
stretched a road which to the left leads to a small village, on the
right straight to the enemy lines. As the road was only about 150

meters away, we could see it pretty clearly. At about eight o'clock ne morning we heard the suspicious sound of motors. It meant a ank attack by the Moors. Hand grenades were ready and in place, ast minute instructions were issued. We had just manned our gun posts when a truck suddenly came down the road. A passenger car ollowed, then again a truck and a third, a fourth and a fifth. From he first line Eberhardt yelled, "Don't shoot, can't you see that it is a green car. They've blundered." None of us could understand why he five trucks should expose themselves that way. But before you knew it one of our boys had fired. A shrouded figure sprung from the foremost truck and plunged into the trenches on our side for cover. A Moor! And then a murderous fire was released on the trucks. Out hey sprang and scampered away like hares. One over there! Bang! Bang! Bang! Another under the truck! Bang! Doggone it, that one got away!

The rear trucks were manoeuvering to get away. Bang! Bang! Trees obstruct our aim and two trucks manage to escape. The other three are stuck. Sudden quiet, except for potshots aimed at their tires. An order is passed around. Again we hear the noise of motors. More trucks, or tanks? Two enemy tanks heave into view. They fire. One salvo after another rattles against our breastworks, like hail. But our trenches give excellent protection and now and again we peek through the holes to see if they have come any closer. It seems not. They are circling around the trucks, figuring out the best way to tow them away. One now takes up a position, throwing us samples of his wares, while the other continues manoeuvering around. Now our mine-thrower goes into action. Shot number one explodes only 10 meters from the first tank. The second shot gets closer. An order comes through from the rear. *Our* tanks are coming! Prepare shock troop with hand grenades! Come on, fellers, hurry while the enemy tanks are still there. Come on! We're on pins and needles. But the forward tank is making off and the further one, too. "Cowards!" we say to ourselves and we feel like leaving the trenches and going after them. But their damn MG's keep pegging away without a break. The next five minutes seem an hour *and then* we hear the rasp of our first tank as it lumbers up behind us. Its revolving gun threatens the hill opposite. And now a second, and a third and a fourth. We call out at them although we know they

can't hear us. Down our hill they rumble and as we follow them wit
our eyes we feel like shouting in Franco's face: "Come ahead, sho
your colors now!" And for sheer joy we fill the air with all sorts o
nonsensical shouts. Hours later we found out that on our right win
the Moors had advanced with a cordon of ten tanks and had com
within three meters of our trenches; that a shock troop of twenty
five of our men had been surrounded by the fascists and all but tw
cut down and that *another* shock troop had gone forward with ou
tanks, got as far as the enemy line, and on returning to our trenche
took the Moors by surprise and drenched them in their own blood

We continued for five days in the same position but the Moor
never dared show their faces again.

And now to wind up, because if I keep writing you may imagin
we have entered Burgos already. It's not as easy as all that. True
we are better equipped than we were, but there's still lots of roor
for improvement. The Madrid front is not the only one. With burn
ing impatience we await the day when the peoples of Europe wi
wake up to realize where the danger lies, and will resume norma
commercial relations with the Republic of Spain. In order that thi
may be realized, you must help.

Best regards from all the boys in our company.

Yours,

WILI

↔

*HANS MARCHWITZA is 57. As a young man he worked as a ston
carrier in the mountains of Upper Silesia in Germany. Later h
became active in the Labor press in Germany and published severa
works in that country before the advent of Hitler forced him to flee int
exile.*

. . . I can give you some really good news. Our Internationa
Brigade has some more very successful weeks behind it. Again th
complete abandon and the unceasing bravery of our Internationa
comrades compel all my admiration. The enemy fears their attacks
that is what the deserters to our side and the prisoners always tel
us.

It is the most beautiful Spring here. A marvellous sun, the field ull of flowers and in our old, tumbledown little farmhouse there are ven a few swallows about, they are building their nest right above ur heads, without paying any attention to us. The war makes one aw, nevertheless many among us look on musingly while the industrious birds give themselves unconcernedly to their family task.

Just now a few flyers dropped their greetings, that is an everyday occurrence already and warns us only that there still is a war nd that this pretty picture of Spring should not deceive us. Let us ope that we shall soon be able to enjoy a real and earned peace. ranco has been squeezed into a defensive more and more and has een forced into a panicky rout on several fronts. Terror is ever nore noticeable and comprehensible in the ranks of his troops, the oldiers whom he forces into his service really don't know what they hould lay down their lives for. Constantly the realization that they re being misused becomes stronger with them and whole groups lesert him to come over to us.

I want to tell you a little story yet very moving. One evening several of their deserters are brought in. Clean-cut, lively farmer lads. I leave them in the care of two of our sentries. One of the sentries takes a look at their faces and says: "Three of them are from my province, I always recognize them right away." Then it really turns out that one of the deserters belongs to the same town as the sentry. The sentry's face clouds and he begins to tell how the fascists have carried on on his native soil. They shot fifteen hundred, his mother who wouldn't betray the hiding place of her youngest son, among them.

The deserter listens, speechless, and with growing excitement. Then he begins to shiver. The sentry breaks off his story, pulls off his cape with a quick and exceptionally beautiful gesture and throws it to the deserter: "Cover yourself," he said, and helps the other one who still hesitates: "Even so we are brothers. You can't help it."

Almost every day one experiences such things over and over again. There is something so big underneath it all and it proves to us that Franco is getting himself more and more into hot water with his dastardly game. Over countless obstacles leads the road to understanding and unity for these sorely tried people. However, they will find themselves united and will chase Franco out of the country. Today we can say calmly: "Our victory is certain. . ."

HANNES

89

From Spanish Trenches

ARNOLD—German Emigré

December 26, 1937

Dear Comrades:

I want to take the opportunity which I have today and give you some idea of what we do on leave. At noon on the 25th of December the emergency had passed and the Edgar André battalion was given leave for town, but not before our battalion commander, to the great delight of all, had informed us that the fascists had been beaten back a full five kilometers all along our front. This again gave proof that the Spaniards are capable of the greatest deeds with discipline and heroism in face of the well equipped Moors and German fascists.

And so the word came: "Back to Madrid," and for one day we felt we need have no fear of the enemy planes, as our anti-aircraft guns are now doing fine work and fascist airmen prefer bombarding the roads out of Madrid where they are beyond reach of the guns and can drop Hitler's Christmas gifts . . . which they insist on distributing.

Pat, Harry and myself had just had our pictures taken and were strutting down the Gran Via to the Capitol. We bought tickets for a good movie and arranged to meet at the theatre at five o'clock. Then we stepped into one of the many Madrid cafés, where Pat went off, leaving only Harry and me together. Suddenly a loud clatter outside. Our first thought was planes. We jumped to our feet to go and see what we could do to help. We looked outside and twenty yards to our right saw a building crashed through by heavy artillery. Into the cloud of dust we rushed to rescue what there was left to rescue. The first thing I saw was human bodies, mangled, smashed to bits, and stout-hearted men carrying the wounded to an ambulance truck. This was Mr. Franco's Christmas present to the people of Madrid, after General Faupel, whom Hitler had placed at his disposal, had recommended he should reduce Madrid to ashes.

But this was only the overture. When I saw that there was nothing to do but to clear up the wreckage I began to think of my own safety. Artillery fire can be calculated pretty accurately. So Harry and I counted and as we did so watched a family group

90

nearby. A father was comforting his frightened child who was trembling all over. We counted and watched for two minutes, and boom! Down I dropped. But nothing. I could turn round to look a few yards away where we had been standing two minutes ago. All I saw was dust and confusion. The Spanish family had disappeared. I hope nothing happened to them.

And now began a scene which I won't forget as long as I live. The civilians were all hurrying for some temporary shelter, mostly into the subway. The Militiamen were bravely rendering first aid and the ambulances kept coming all the time. The fire engines came, too, and everything was handled in such a calm and ordered manner that you would think it had been rehearsed. Harry and I agreed that the bombardment was intended for the telephone building across the way, as the immediate objective, but that the deeper motive of the fascists was to terrorize the people of Madrid. For this reason they launched their fire at 3:30 in the afternoon when most people are out for a walk. Volley followed volley. Harry and I separated and I decided to go to the subway, like the others. I was on my way down when a sense of shame, because of the uniform I was wearing, held me back and I went up into the street again. I could only watch helplessly as the incendiary bombs, one after the other, exploded on roofs and thoroughfares. I kept looking on impersonally and observed how the whole crowd of pedestrians sought their safety with orderliness and method. Even to the way in which they threw themselves flat on the ground. At 5:30 the bombardment stopped and the streets took on their normal appearance again.

I had to break my appointment as it would have been crazy to attempt to negotiate those 500 yards at that time.

I haven't yet found out what damage actually was done on Christmas day, but I do know this: that Franco will never succeed in undermining the spirit of the Madrileños by subjecting Madrid to artillery fire. Recent weeks have demonstrated that the people of Madrid will grit their teeth and hold out. I know, for I have seen that they do not know what panic is and that they gird themselves to the defense of Madrid with all the more pluck and determination. This, comrades, means something when you remember the 3000 and odd wounded civilians caused by air raids alone (bombs of German make, fragments were found with German trademark!).

Such is the peace and happiness which Franco wants to bring the Spanish people. It is up to you now, comrades, to show in even greater measure than before your solidarity with the Spanish people. Work within your organizations, work among the masses to have the blockade against Spain lifted. Franco's hirelings must be beaten. To defeat Franco is to defeat Hitler and Mussolini. Today we must remember the bodies shot to fragments in the city of Madrid and must dedicate ourselves anew to bring about fascism's defeat before fascism bring on the horror of a greater World War. The best way to slake Hitler of his war-fever is by winning here and now.

That's all. I go back to the front. The dream "Reserves are resting" is over. We go back without hesitation, with the determination to hold our ground. We shall do our duty until death!

Yours,

ARNOLD

↔

FRITZ MUENSTER, exiled from Germany, lived in Holland previous to his departure for the front in Spain.

January 26, 1937

My dear Comrade and friends!

It was an exceptional pleasure to receive your letter, I have read it several times, everything you tell me seems so far away.

Joop is right when he ascribes world-significance to the battle in Spain. To me the question of the defense of the democratic rights of a people has never been so clear as just at this time that I am in Spain. Even more impressive and tremendous, yes, gigantic, is the incredible, enormous bond of the entire International Proletariat. Be it little Holland, be it Germany, America, no matter where we are, in the trenches or under fire, we have the workers of all countries on our side. Hans Niessen and I are on a gun (machine gun division), both of us have been recommended for promotion, Hans and I to officers. It is a big honor of course to work for our proletarian army. Just now Hans is division leader of a M.G. division

nd I have been ordered to a post about which I cannot write you
anything. But Hans and I always are the best of pals and in the fire
f the battle, our friendship has become much stronger. Some days
go, I met several comrades from Amsterdam here and the recol-
ections became real lively. Notwithstanding all these painful, great
acrifices, our determination and the knowledge of the final victory
ave become much stronger. And why? Certainly we have the very
est of our people here but the Spanish people are even more admirable and endearing in their confidence of victory. Boys! The
Spanish youth (of the Popular Front) fight for victory with the love
f their country and the conviction, that they have chased all the
ld feudalistic vermin to the devil — their love to us Germans has
often moved me to tears. Only one example! Our Thaelmann Bat-
alion near Madrid had some very hot days behind it. All Madrid
was very concerned about our Thaelmann Battalion and when we
were lucky enough to come out from the fighting for a rest period
n the neighbourhood of Madrid, we were received by the Madrid
comrades with a great joy and enthusiasm, such as I have seldom
experienced. I am going to give you just one example of that. At
Christmas time we got a package as a holiday gift from the Spanish
organizations. In my package there was a letter in the Spanish language written by a Spanish family, who wished me a happy Christmas and invited me to visit them when I came to Madrid.

As we went back to the front on the third holiday, I could only
thank them by letter and tell them, that, if I returned from the
front in good health, I would visit them. When we had those hard
days behind us, I hurried to make my visit to Madrid. Hans and I
were received as though we were long-lost sons, the whole afternoon
we were on the go with our Spanish friends and when our autos
came and we had to go back to our company, I got a surprise. Our
Spanish comrades gave me a gold seal ring, a fountain pen and an
awful lot of candy and chocolate, which we devoured with our
comrades on our two hour auto trip.

Now that we are far away from Madrid, I often get letters and
post cards. They ask me to stay in Spain, they think that the
fascists will be beaten in May and that the time of quiet and peace
will come for Spain then too.

Boys! Don't be angry if my letter is muddled. because while I am

93

writing to you I get the news that a Spanish and a Belgian comrad
fell. They were with me in the machine gun division and were ver
dear to me. You never feel the loss of people who are dear to you a
strongly as in the war. But however painful it is, we are a fast-livin,
generation.

Now I want to close in the hope that my letter reaches you an
that you will answer it again. The best to all of you and to ou,
Dutch friends. Many sincere greetings and wishes from your friend

FRITZ

*BODO UHSE is about thirty years old. Yet he is older in experience.
Before he reached his sixteenth birthday he was active in the fascist
movement in Germany under the leadership of Hitler. Later, however,
he became interested in the Agrarian movement of the German Social-
Democrats. He was exiled in 1933. His book, published in Switzerland
in 1934, and titled "Mercenary and Soldier," lost him the citizenship
of the country of his birth.*

Somewhere in Spain a very young German died a horrible death.
One of his countrymen, his enemy in life, who witnessed his death,
wrote the following words in his memory:

Some time ago a German pursuit plane, which had taken part in
an attack on our lines, fell to the ground. The pilot tried to save
himself by a parachute-jump, but was attacked by the German
plane which had accompanied him and was killed by machine gun
bullets. His corpse landed within the lines of the republican army.
He carried no papers. On the inside of his belt they found the
words: Private Franke.

The private must have been very young. We do not know his
exact age. We have no ground to suppose that he had not been a
decent and law-abiding citizen during his lifetime, like many, who
give their good faith to a bad cause and really only make themselves guilty by not thinking. When Franke really had the opportunity to meditate on his life for the first time, and also really
had reason to do so, it was already too late for him. His last active
enterprise was the jump from the falling machine. After the eter-

nally long seconds of the fast fall he dangled comfortably under the yellow silken sky of his parachute and floated down will-lessly, while the wind drove him ever farther behind the lines of the government troops.

He had nothing to do, he could meditate. What he was thinking, we do not know, because it was not possible for him to tell anyone about it later. But the thoughts of a soldier are simple. Surely he started by cursing his rotten luck and he probably cursed the motor of his plane, rightfully so, and, to be sure, he was not the only one, nor was it the first time that his motor abandoned him. The private probably did not know that his highest in command, that marvelous General Goering, owned stock in the plane factory, which builds such incapable and untrustworthy machine as the H54, otherwise he would no doubt have burdened his Brigadier-General with all the oaths at his command. One thing we can be sure of though: that Franke cursed the whole expedition to Spain in this moment and that he regretted it too. But he did not reproach himself in this fatal monologue, because it had not been within his power to make this trip or to stay at home: it had been recommended to him.

Of course Franke's next thought had turned to the vain hope that the wind might get a sudden impulse to turn around and waft him toward the positions of the rebels. But the wind did not turn, the parachute continued unperturbed on its trip toward the earth. Inactive, left to the hand of fate, Franke surely thought of relatives, of his parents, friends and some young girl. He must have tried to figure out what would become of him after he landed, too.

It is in these meditations that he was disturbed. Close to him his comrade, who had seen his machine fall and who had seen him bail out, dived out of the clouds. The plane came — as could be observed from the ground — to about one hundred yards of the parachute. Franke must have remembered — not without fright — the order which he had received shortly before going up. This order was that any comrade, who was in danger, through any circumstance of falling into enemy hands, must be killed irrevocably.

This order was the result of some handbills, that planes of our side had thrown down a few days ago, showing the pictures of two of their comrades, and with their handwritten explanation that

95

they were forced to land in enemy territory, had been taken prisoner, and were treated well by the republicans. Attached to this message there had been the remark: the fight against the Spanish people was not serving a good cause.

The private must have realized — seeing the machine of his comrade and remembering the order — that there was only one chance to save his life, and that was to fall into the hands of the enemy. The pilot of the other plane, who was no stranger to Franke, but one of his comrades, whom he knew by name and with whom he had already emptied many a glass, began to fire at Franke, who was hanging doomed and helpless from his parachute, slowly dangling toward the earth.

As far as could be observed, the first shots did not find their target. The plane continued on its way, the cramp, which had attacked Franke's stomach and had curled his whole body up into a knot, let go of him, and for seconds the private had time to curse his comrade, who really held himself to the scandalous order. He must have promised himself never again to participate in such dastardly "schweinerei." He wished that his parachute might fall faster, he wished he were a prisoner already.

When he had come flying along in the morning, the republicans had been his enemies, now the rescue could only come from them, and the enemy, the deathly enemy, was his comrade of this morning! The fall of Franke from the clouds to the earth was a fall of falsehood to truth. He recognized that a cause which drove its followers to such scandalous actions, could not be good; he understood that he was the victim of murder for murder's sake.

The plane of his comrade returned. It circled around the parachute. The machine gun fired incessantly. Perhaps Franke still had time for one last curse, which must yet be ringing in Hitler's ears.

When the parachute settled on the earth, private Franke was dead, his body was a sieve, machine gun bullets had torn through it everywhere.

ENGLAND

DAVID COOK was born and raised in the south of England. He finished school and came to the United States when he was about 21 years old to make his first million dollars.

He was rather appalled and surprised when he found that this would not be easy if he had to work his way up from a shipping clerk in a New York firm, where he found employment.

Without any resources, he enrolled at Columbia University and managed to graduate after four years of hard studying, earning a living at all the odd jobs that a college student finds time to do.

In Columbia University he became interested in the student movement. He wanted to help other youths to a better chance for a college education.

He had gone back to England to live with his family when the military rebellion in Spain urged him to drop everything until the fascists had been defeated and the Spanish people assured of the right to live by the government of their choice.

The letters which follow are to a former college friend and co-worker in the student movement.

January 24, 1937

Dear Jimmy:

Left London January 2nd, about 150 of us split in small batches. The group was ninety per cent proletarian in composition, a large proportion of Scotsmen. We came through Paris, crossed the border into Catalonia; passed through Barcelona and Valencia. We crossed the border with hardly any trouble except for a few hours' formal delay. At Paris we had our first touch of the international aspects of the undertaking — Germans who had escaped, Czechs, Dutchmen, Austrians — the exiles had left for the front long before. My French came in handy as we were terribly short of interpreters and before long I found myself escorting a couple of hundred well-assorted anti-fascists to the border and rushing around talking fluent but inferior German, French and pigeon English in all directions.

From Spanish Trenches

Over the border this situation was intensified. We put up at an enormous fort for a couple of days. In one huge vaulted cellar with navy beds as a municipal lodging house, it was a real Babel. There we were whipped into some sort of temporary organization prior to leaving for the base. Life in the town seemed quite tranquil, good relations appearing to exist between all left-wing parties. This is noteworthy since, as you probably know, the fear once existed in certain groups that we were coming to Spain not merely to defeat fascism. These fears are now more or less dissipated, I believe, for the role of the Brigade in saving Madrid would be hard to over-estimate.

We got to Barcelona on a little single track line railway which averaged about twenty m.p.h. and arrived after six hours. We were met by a band at the station and paraded triumphantly through the streets to the barracks where we had lunch. Still no signs of war — but a peculiar electrically equalitarian atmosphere. Cheering, the clenched fist salute, smiles and shouts. Sometimes a mother holding a baby in her arms would take its sticky fist from its mouth and hold its arm up in the clenched fist salute — what sort of a generation will this political precocity produce? No one ever uses the word *señor*, only *camarade* — and one feels that it is not mere expediency. Passing the Martini-Rossi Vermouth factory, the salute again from women workers looking out the window. Park Avenue would boycott the stuff if it only knew.

We were in Barcelona only a couple of hours, ushered out again to the station. Louis Fischer and Hans Eisler were both on the train with us to Valencia. I had always visualized Fischer as a scholarly, shrivelled up little academician and was astounded at this walloping, great tough.

The journey from Barcelona to Valencia was bad. Spanish time estimates are never especially accurate but we were told we'd arrive there between 9 and 10 P.M., yet didn't get in until 4 A.M. Fuel shortage due to blockade, I suppose. Still, nothing more extreme than this was not so bad under the circumstances. Then on to ——— [name removed by censor] where we arrived on January 7th.

We had been travelling for five days, continually on the move and little time for political or military organization. We were all

98

thirsting for news, too, as once in Spain we seemed far less informed than before — an occasional old copy of *Humanité* being all we could get hold of.

One is struck here, as in England, by the size and grandeur of the Church, contrasted with the homes of local villagers. Religious feeling never ran high here — that is in the last few years. Even the more conservative element was apparently Republican. Now that the priests have been accessory to the murder of their own congregations, what little religious enthusiasm there was has diminished.

At mealtimes the family crouches on low stools around an open fire in the kitchen-dining room and eats from a communal bowl. Only one spoon is used — not to put in the mouth but to spread the food on bread. Each family makes its own wine, most using bare feet as a press. The women stick to housework, never smoke, and although at times they work in the field, the idea of their joining the union seems to be unheard of. There are a mass of similar contradictions due to the short time in which political development has been concentrated. The greatest contradiction of all is precisely the degree of political advancement with the most primitive material — considerable illiteracy, no plumbing, mud-puddles for roads. Craftsmanship especially in metal is of a very high order, however. Culturally life here is absolutely stagnant. They spend their leisure merely sitting around the fire. The job of material and cultural reconstruction here will be as great as in the U.S.S.R. and similar, I imagine, in many respects.

It's days since I left off writing this. An example of our democracy: T. H. Wintringham is out here. As a technical expert he rates about second in command of the battalion. One night a group was in the club-room, a large place, small tables for writing, chess, a counter to sell cigarettes, stove in the middle, wall-newspaper, radio. A group was listening to the news coming over — news is a luxury here so send along copies of the N.M. please. Wintringham came striding in asking for Comrade So-and-So. He interfered with reception of the news. Immediately with no hesitation, the whole bunch of us rank-and-filers silenced him indignantly. He crept out like a mouse.

The armory was previously the priest's house. Like all the

houses of wealthy people, it was commandeered during the highly advisable absence of the owners. One afternoon we were stripping our machine gun, which we nurse like a new-born babe, and looked around for some ways of keeping the small parts free from dust and grit. Someone, from somewhere, produced a beautifully embroidered tablecloth, all handwork, with the name Sofia worked into one corner. Carefully it was spread on the ground. We kept our muddy boots off it, but placed the barrel-end in the middle, and all the greasy parts over the rest. It all seemed to smack most strongly of poetic justice.

Before coming out here I edited one issue of the University Labour Federation magazine. Out here I'm having a shot at editing the wall—newspaper, though I'd never seen one in my life. It's interesting work. Copy contains a good deal of semi-humorous self-criticism — of drunkenness, of indiscriminate excretion in unsuitable places, fighting among ourselves. Others contrast the Spaniards' material backwardness with their political advancement. They cite the difference between ourselves and a Red Army — the point that we are here to defend democracy, not set up Soviets. They report the heightening of military efficiency by political understanding — voluntary self-discipline as opposed to that which is imposed from above. A lot of it is on a slightly bawdy plane, but the masses are not fastidious.

On the 25th we held a Burns night. The proportion of Scots is extremely high — Glasgow being one of the most politically advanced cities in Great Britain. It was an astonishing event. About 150 people — seventy per cent Scots — in the café of the Republican club. Tickets were taken at the door by sentries with rifles. Up in the hall, on the second floor, posters flooded the walls. Though there is not a printed copy of one of Burns' poems in the place, they gave excellent talks on Burns as poet of the poverty-stricken Scottish peasantry, on his revolutionary equalitarianism, his support of the French revolution and international outlook — all so closely resembling our own presence in Spain. There were recitals of some poems; popular chorus of Scottish songs, musical turns in which were used an accordion which had seen service up in the lines; a phoney violin loaned by the local Popular Front; spoons used as castanets. The orchestra alternated between Scottish ballads and revolutionary songs. A few had kilts on, which created a sensation among the Spaniards. For the feast every man brought his own mess tins. Some of us ate sardines with the aid of bayonets. Never has there been such a Burns night — never has the occasion been celebrated more truly in the spirit of the life and works of the man being honored.

I don't believe any of us — at least those who have not been to the front — think much about death, certainly so far as the guns are concerned. The target is regarded as an impersonal objective; the purpose of the guns purely as a technique to be mastered.

One of the leaders here is a naval gunner, kicked out in the Invergordon mutiny in 1934. There is one other sailor, full of guts, devil-may-care, impatient of discipline but keen and quick on the uptake, efficient in his work though superficially slipshod. Two Scotch coal miners, one government aircraft worker, one unemployed laborer, one extraordinary fellow, a hobo who in my opinion is a case of dementia praecox; one engineer.

Then an old fellow of sixty-two whose two sons have followed him here. He is fighting for the future of the coming generation. All are honest to God British proletarian types.

I came here because life in England was too useless a one to be living at such a time as this. If I'm to be among those who don't get back, I'll have concentrated so much into the last short space that it will be as good as having lasted for a normal span.

This bloody letter has gone on long enough. A letter means a tremendous lot here so please write and get anyone else to do so if you can. I don't guarantee to reply promptly but conditions permitting I will drop you a line. All the very best to you all — The ASU and the Youth Congress. Let's know if there is anyone out here from the U.S. whom I know.

Don't forget to write. DAVE

April 22, 1937

Dear Jimmy:

Receiving letters, some letters, can yield an extraordinary keen pleasure, so take this "Thank you" as something more than a mere formality.

From Spanish Trenches

Conditions here don't permit well-organized correspondence or flowing prose. For one thing there is so much to write that a letter is simply not the correct medium. What's needed is a social history which I shall not inflict on you at this moment.

The feeling of being neither flesh nor fish, which so many of us in the middle class know only too well, is resolved over here. There are occasional discouragements, disappointments, shattering of false ideas — but those which one retains are all the stronger, in fact, tougher. And as soon as one sees this war in its historical framework one is filled with a feeling of tremendous pride, as well as a joy and gratification at the privilege of taking part in it. It is no false modesty which makes me feel that it is probably much easier to be here than elsewhere, that in a sense it needs less courage to be within 200 metres of the fascist lines than it does to stay at home. It is a sort of war and peace which passeth all understanding. There is a danger of becoming priggish, like a saint who knows his own salvation is assured . . .

Recovering from wounds took about seven weeks during the last two of which I did almost nightly broadcasts of news to England for ten minutes at a time. After that, back to the front. Without any mock-heroics, it was in many ways a pleasure to return. One had less of a feeling of uselessness; it was good to see old friends. Life becomes a pretty concentrated business when you're not at all sure just how much of it is left. Friendships built up in a month or two become deep.

Things were very different when we first went up. Then it was a matter of advancing over open country. Now there are trenches, the whole scene has an air of solidity and permanence. As a matter of fact I was back less than a week, during which things were pretty quiet except for a successful attack made by our flanking battalions. I have now been recalled, along with others, for special training. On this it is naturally impossible to enlarge, except that it is in keeping with the changed character of the war and the corresponding change of role which we in the International Brigades are called on to play.

This change is by far the most astounding thing that I've seen happen here. The life of the whole country is today concentrated in exactly the same way as that of the individual. In this boiling point

102

of Spanish history one can see some qualitative changes going on in one's daily experience. The relative chaos, the whole haphazard spirit, some entirely false estimates of the situation, which only a few months ago were prevalent in some circles, are rapidly fading away. In a short time the whole nation will not only be in arms; it will be a nation of trained soldiers with the economic bases and the social relations which are essential to its support and success. That's a far cry from the romantic, courageous and none too effective army in overalls which existed before. In this transformation both the military organization and the political structure of the Brigades have been important.

There's a quiet confidence here now. The testing period is over and there's no holding us down any more. Spain will come out of this soon and with flying colors. She's lived to set up a technical, military and economic machine which can now compare with that of her opponents. And to top off the material accomplishment she has such overwhelming superiority on the spiritual side that the outcome is not for a moment in doubt.

Salud!

DAVE

THE SOVIET UNION

ILYA GRIGORYEVICH ERENBURG does not represent the Russian government in the short articles which follow. His experiences in Spain are those of a man who loves the country and its people, who has traveled there often and who has written more than one book about Spain.

Erenburg was born of bourgeois parents in 1891. Early enthusiasm swept him into the revolutionary underground movement of Czarist Russia. He tired of this, deserted the revolution and its cause, left Russia for France where he became interested in mysticism through his contacts with cultists there. We find him back in the Soviet state from 1917 to 1921. He is a cynic; he ridicules the ideals of the Revolution as well as he ridicules the western bourgeoisie and capitalism. He merely scoffs and offers no remedy. His innate individualism endears the Spanish people, individualists like himself, to him.

Patiently the Soviet presses print his anti-Soviet verse. He may not believe in Communism nor in the creative power of the proletariat, but as long as he does not advocate rebellion against the dictatorship of the proletariat, they are content with merely criticizing his writings.

In 1921 he returned abroad and only saw his fatherland on occasional short visits. His novel "Julio Jurenito," printed in Moscow in 1928 unleashed a storm of literary protest.

It seemed that the implicit faith of the Soviet people in their government at last found its reward.

In recent years Erenburg has come to identify himself as writer and man with Soviet letters and life.

Toledo

It was a hot and sultry Spanish summer day. The earth seemed naked and rusty. Tiny villages blended with the earth. The houses were without windows: life was hiding from the crazy sun. We were making our way past barricades made up of barrels, flour sacks and straw. On a corn-kiln nearby I saw an inscription: "We shall break General Cabanella's neck."

104

From an earthen jug a peasant was pouring a thin stream of precious water into his wide open mouth. He offered me the jug: "Drink, Russian." With an old hunting rifle in his hand, he was standing guard — alone amidst the heat and silence. His sons had been shot by the fascists.

For quite a long time we were riding through the stony desert of Aragon. We moved very slowly. At each turn we would stop and ask: "Who is farther on? Our people? They?" The peasants answered pathetically and confusedly. They demanded rifles. Young fellows, their fists raised high were saying: "They shall not pass." One peasant, exposing his bare chest, pierced the air with his pitchfork and replied: "Farther on? Farther on is — war."

The villages were disappearing. The heaps of stones on the road seemed like some pre-historic architecture. The darkness was growing thicker. Heat-lightning streaked the black sky. In the distance, cannon began to roar. Suddenly our automobile stopped: A barricade was barring the way. We looked about. There wasn't a soul around. All our searches were in vain. Finally, among the cliffs, I noticed a shadow appear and disappear. Some one began to curse angrily: "Pass word?" We replied: "Vigilance for all." We did not know the pass word of this section. We repeated an old pass word used in a different section. The stones around us remained silent. I asked Jaime, my fellow traveller: "Who do you think they might be?" He took out his gun from his holster. The men upon the cliff were aiming at us with rifles. Suddenly the militiaman who was sitting on the seat next to the chauffeur began to curse. He put his gun aside and walked over alone to the cliff. We soon heard his voice: "To the devil, these are our people!" The peasants began to laugh gaily. "And we thought you were fascists," one of them said. "We've been here for six nights."

"Where is the front now?" I asked.

They did not know. As far as they were concerned the front was everywhere. A cool breeze dispersed the sultriness. The peasants wrapped themselves tighter in their blankets.

"Go to sleep," said Jaime.

"No," they replied, "we must be on the lookout."

They told us that there were four fascists in their village. One old peasant, spitting in disgust, mentioned them all by name. Their

landowner was a marquis and his manager used to rape little girls
And their priest, while escaping from the wrath of the village in
habitants, lost his golden cross and a lady's brooch near the mill.

They told us with pride of their new threshing-machine, recently
acquired. When they confiscated the marquis' land they organized
their own "kolkhoz." An old peasant said: "Do you know how much
the manager used to pay us for a day's work? Fifty centimes. We
ate meat only at weddings. And now . . ." He clutched his rifle
tighter. "They came on Sunday," he continued. "One, dressed in
civilian clothes, cried out: 'In the name of Jacob' — that's their
pass word. They shot Ramon. They killed two mules. But we shot
back at them and they had to beat it . . ."

The old man gave me a friendly pat on the back. "It is only
twelve kilometers to Bujaralos," he said. "The pass word is: 'All
rifles to the front.'"

When we were getting ready to leave a young fellow appeared
from the darkness. Rubbing his eyes with his fists, he exclaimed in
parting: "They shall not pass." Perhaps that was Ramon's son.

In Toledo the wife of a fascist officer attempted to get out of the
Alcazar with her two children. She ran out to the Square. The militiamen lowered their rifles. A shot was heard: a white guard had
killed the wife of his own comrade. The children ran over to the
militiamen. One boy was ten, the other eight years old. The grim-
looking militiamen who greet each other with "Greetings and dyna-
mite" gently lifted these two boys and the working women of
Toledo brought them milk.

Six gendarmes succeeded in escaping from the fortress at night.
Their faces had a deathly pallor and their voices were scarcely audi-
ble: It seemed as though they had forgotten how to speak. They
told me about the curse of the Alcazar. When a fascist airplane
would throw provisions to the beleaguered the officers would eat the
ham but to the gendarmes they would say: "Be brave." They
drove out hostages and laughed at their fear: "Brothers killing
brothers." They buried the dead in the stables.

The militiamen placed a loudspeaker on the square but their
words never reached the Alcazar. All that the beleaguered heard
were the martial strains of the march "Riego" interrupted by the
cries of the insane.

The Government proposed to the Whites to free the women and children. The Whites refused: they played upon the soft-heartedness of the republicans. Instead the fascists requested hypocritically: "Send us a priest, we want to pray before our death." The government sent a priest to the Alcazar. The priest said to the fascists: "Let out your wives and children." The fascists replied: "We shall all die together." The priest said: "Let out the wives and children of the militiamen whom you have captured on the streets." The fascists replied: "They shall die with us." The priest saw what baseness meant and after leaving the Alcazar, raised his fist and said to the militiamen, "Greetings, comrades."

While negotiations were going on, at the entrance of the half-ruined Alcazar, the enemies met: white guard officers and militiamen. An officer said: "You are scoundrels."

The workers replied: "No, you are scoundrels."

"We are defending an ideal."

The militiamen began to laugh: "We are fighting for an ideal. We want happiness for all but you want happiness for your own gang."

The officer thought for a while and replied: "Our gang is superior to yours."

The workers did not reply. They merely grasped their rifles more firmly.

After a moment's silence the officer said: "You are smoking, we haven't smoked for a long time."

The militiamen offered their cigarettes to the fascists . . .

A government airplane was getting ready to bombard the Alcazar. The militiamen were told: "Stand at a distance of 100 meters."

The militiamen replied: "No, they might run away." Fourteen militiamen were killed during this aerial bombardment. Not one of them moved away. They were sitting on their straw chairs with their rifles ready: they were waiting for the beast that was being smoked out from his lair.

They were laying mines under the Alcazar. A militiaman showed me an entrance to an underground passage and said: "That's where I work." He had gray hair from the dust and black young eyes. It was a hot and sultry day. The guns were silent, the people were silent — silence all around. After a moment of meditation, the militiamen said: "I have there a wife and two children. I can't tell you anything about the wife: A woman can betray. And one can betray a woman. But do you know what this means?" . . . He took out from his pocket a photograph, covered with dust. I saw two little girls, dressed up in Sunday clothes. He replaced the photograph, turned his head aside and said: "Now we shall make quick work of them." Without looking at me any further, he commenced to work again.

Barcelona

In the beginning of the civil war General Franco sent the flyer Iturbi to bomb the republican positions. On the way Iturbi killed the two officers who accompanied him and landed in Madrid. He was congratulated, they wanted to fête him. He answered: "Let us start fighting in a hurry."

For two months he flew pursuit planes, defended open cities and forced the whites to the ground. He did what tens of his comrades did. When they told him: "You are a hero" he answered: "I am a flyer."

On September 13th four planes bombarded the republican positions in the Santa Olalla sector. The pursuit planes of the rebels surrounded Iturbi. He threw himself at one of the enemy planes. The charred remains of the big and genial fellow fell to the ground.

From the plane brought down by Iturbi a flyer made a parachute jump. When he reached the earth he was surrounded by militiamen. The scared rebel aviator cried with a foreign accent: "Comrades, don't kill me!" They took him to Madrid. All the way he held his fist up. He was an Italian, twenty-three years old. He told a long and detailed story of how much pay the white Generals gave to the different hirelings. He calculated it all in pesetas, dollars and lires. He complained of the crying injustice that others were paid better than he. When they offered him a bottle of lemonade, he began to believe in life again, and lowered his fist. He was asked how he had come to take service with Franco. They expected long tirades about glorious Italy, about the Duce and fascism. But no, when he had finished his lemonade he began to speak about pesetas, dollars and lires again. He knew only one thing: the representative of the Fiat automobile factory had promised him more.

It was a hard day: the regiments of *regulares* advanced from Talavera in the direction of Magueda. I remembered the fate of Iturbi and then the large headlines of the newspapers: "We shall be victorious" seemed like a simple and absolute truth.

A spirit of gayety pervaded the barracks. The 19th of July column was leaving for the front.

The children thought that the shining caps of their fathers were splendid. Women held their men in a tight embrace. Every now and then a moment of quiet would steal into the festive mood. Eyes sparkled. A young girl repeated over and over: ". . . You *will* write to me, won't you . . ." A skinny young fellow clasped his gun tightly and talked, nobody knew to whom: "A gun, but that has to be cleaned, doesn't it? . . ." I heard a little old woman whisper to her son: "Shall I go all the way to the station with you? Can I?" That wasn't a scene from a movie, that was real.

The Germans marched in the front. They carried the portrait of Thaelmann. Blond, blue eyed, bigger than the others; they know how to march too. They looked like masters of the military art. They had known much sorrow: the downfall, jail, solitude, the tortures of their exile. Among these happy, fiery and brave men, in the company of their bravery and childlike good humor they had regained their hope. They went to the bastions of Saragossa to save the sons of Pomerania and Baden. They smiled happily at the noisy Barcelenos who greeted the departing column from their balconies.

The little grandmother marched at the side of her son. The column dissolved into the crowd; a woman marched at the side of every man. It is the warmth of a full life, which makes death easy. Only the Germans marched alone, their manly gait was a soldier's gait. They were foreigners in this fair country. When the column crossed the Rambla — I saw two factory girls. They went toward the Germans hesitantly and without saying a word; just smiling a bit, they marched at their side.

The red roses were like flames, which shot out from their bayonets.

From Spanish Trenches

Late in the afternoon I arrived in Guadarrama. I thought of the villages in Champagne and Artois in 1916. Guadarrama was nothing but a skeleton.

The holes where windows had been pushed in by grenades showed horrible pictures from everyday life; a child's crib or a mirror. Broken kitchenware spread around everywhere.

From this havoc rose an indescribable sadness, a feeling of nausea, of desolation, of devastation. The Whites were 500 yards away. They held the road under fire and chased fanciful shadows whirling in the pale light of the moon.

They brought a ruddy-faced farmer to the political section of the column. A corporal's stripe of the old army was sewed on the sleeve of his tunic. With four of his buddies he had crossed no man's land. I lit up his face with an end of a candle. He was pale as death. His dull eyes showed only exhaustion. He said, as though he wanted to excuse himself: "The food they had was very bad . . ." His buddies slept behind the wall. When the firing stopped the breathing of the boys seemed heavy and noisy. The corporal told me the story of his flight: "I am an artillery man. We served the 75th battery, over there, on top of the mountain. I have been wanting to come over to our side for a long time now, but I didn't have the chance. We shot badly, we wanted to shoot as far as possible. I told my buddies that our place was on the other side. Three of them came along with me. In the hospital I found a flag, I tore the red from it and hid it. Day before yesterday, it was a Wednesday, I said to the officer: Over there by the windmill there is a calf. I want you to know that the food question was pretty bad; it often happened that we had to live on biscuits for four days in a row. He must have felt like eating a piece of roast meat every bit as much as I did. I gave the high sign to my three comrades, but then Gonzales came tagging along. He never opened his mouth, so that you never knew what went on inside of him. I was thinking to myself, perhaps we will have to get him out of the way. We came to the mill where the calf stood. All at once Gonzales says to me: 'Listen, Pepe, I don't feel like kickin' the bucket . . . On the other side are our people!' We left the calf in the lurch and beat it as fast as we could! . . . I couldn't contain myself, I embraced him . . . I took the red rag from my pocket.

110

They shot at us, but nothin' doin'. I have asked to serve a battery. I know how to take aim."

Probably he had told this story several times already. His voice was dull, as though he were reciting a lesson he had learned. The militiamen listened to him in complete silence. One of them pulled out a piece of sausage, cut off a piece: "Here, Pepe!" Another one brought wine, which made a plopping sound. The militiamen said: "Drink, Pepe; you have to get your strength back."

"What is your name?" I asked the corporal. A militiaman interrupted: "You mustn't write down his name. His family is on the other side." The corporal got red in the face with anger and cried: "No . . ." He took a pencil and wrote his name with long strokes like a vineyardist or a herder. "At a moment like that you can't do otherwise," he said. His voice was overfull. He bent down toward the candle and I saw his glowing eyes. I did not think anymore about the horror of the ruins. In unhappy Guadarrama I learned to know the fraternity of men, love, will and self-sacrifice.

Now I want to tell you about little Tito Gerassi. His parents lived in Paris. On the first day of the civil war his father went to the front. He fought at Irun. Knowing that her place was in Spain, Tito's mother brought him to a children's summer camp. She went to the camp to say goodbye to him. Tito was in seventh heaven: "Will you stay with me long, until tonight? . . ." After which he continued: "All the children are gone already, they say that vacation is over. Tell Father, that he must come back soon." The mother could not contain herself, her eyes were filled with tears. Then Tito Gerassi — the little Spaniard said: "Listen, you better go right away! I will turn around and you too, you turn around. We won't look at each other . . ."

In the midst of naked rocks, under the pitiless, desiccating rays of the sun towered the walls of the Escorial. They were six yards thick. Charles the Fifth wanted to build a palace and he built barracks. Not a tree, not a sprig of grass.

Part of the palace served as a hospital. From Peregrinos or from Guadarrama, past steep and difficult roads, slowly creeping automobiles with dimmed headlights carried away the wounded.

The director of the Tourist service with the Academy button in his buttonhole came toward me. He sighed: "There are no tourists

111

any more. May I tell you something about the history of the Escorial?" I smiled. "Then at least put your signature into the guestbook." In the way in which he stood in front of me he looked like the stone of the Escorial, dead, but stirring. I left him in the lurch and went to the wounded. They lived the battle all over again. They spoke of hand grenades, encounters and victory. I saw a young fellow clench the fist of his left arm; he had lost his right arm at Peregrinos.

From the darkness suddenly came a death rattle. It was a farmer from Avila province with a feverish face and a white beard. A bullet had punctured one of his lungs on a reconnaissance trip. He spoke with difficulty and I thought: "he had better not speak," but he shook his head and started to tell me how he had finally discovered the position of the enemy's machine gun. He had to talk; the doctor had me understand that he couldn't last through the night. My companion asked him: "What organization do you belong to, the C.N.T. or the U.G.T?" The wounded man didn't answer and started to talk about the battle again, about reconnaissances and cannons. "They executed four girls," he said. "We got there toward night . . ." There were two words that he pronounced more clearly than any others. *Nosotros e ellos.* "We and they." With the hand of death on him he was full of life. In this dead and shameful Escorial he was life itself. It wasn't the blood of his wound which choked him, but hate and love. "THEY Shall Not Pass! WE Shall Conquer."

Two weeks later I was in Barcelona. I was present at a meeting which turned into fruitless, embittered and noisy discussion. I was to speak about the defense of Culture. I found myself in the midst of people whose life I did not understand and whose language I followed laboriously. Some yelled: "Long live Anarchistic Communism," and others: "Long live the Republic."

I thought of the wounded farmer at Escorial, his grey hairs and his glowing eyes. I spoke of him on the platform and repeated the two words: Nosotros e Ellos. An enthusiastic howling was their answer. People clasped each other's hands in a brotherly spirit and smiled full of hope. The shadow of the mortally wounded man swept through the enormous hall. One big cry came from a thousand breasts: "NO PASARAN!"

112

IRELAND

*RANK RYAN is the leader of the Irish Battalion in Spain. He is
 ardent Catholic who was born in Limerick County in the early part
 the century. Three of his sisters are nuns, two brothers are physi-
ans, and Frank is the youngest of this family. He was graduated from
e National University in Dublin; became a newspaper editor of such
pers as An Poblacht (The Republic), The Irish People and The
emocrat. He became a member of the I.R.A. in 1918, was so well
ked that he was elected to the executive board of the Gaelic League
d to the presidency of the Sean Cole Gaelic Football Club in
ublin.*

Socoro Rojo, Albacete, Spain, January 3, 1937

Iy dear Gerald:

It's time I thought of writing you — but the trouble is to find a
uiet corner in this country. Every place is full, everybody is rush-
g about. Anyway, here I am. We arrived here the 16th of Decem-
er, five hundred and fifty strong, of which three hundred and fifty
re from Ireland, fifty being from Belfast, sixty Liverpool-Irish,
nd as you know New York, Philadelphia and Boston are well
presented. The Irish lads who had enlisted at the start of the
ostilities and who were attached to the French and British com-
anies of the International Brigade are being transferred to the
rish Battalion.

We are in excellent form, having been in intensive training and
has done us a lot of good. I have sent one Irish unit to the front
n December 28th, and there is another in the making. But
ou must remember that all our years in the I.R.A. were to
ood purpose; these lads are well trained and they will never
t us down. Those who come home from this scrap will be of
ood use in Ireland soon. Quite a lot of our crowd were in the
.R.A. right up to their departure; this will be the making of
hem.

And you should see the International Brigades. There isn't a
ountry that isn't represented and there is great camaraderie, in

113

spite of it all. The trouble is, there aren't enough guns in the coun try. Thousands of Spaniards are not yet armed.

The people are 90% against Franco. I've been among the peas ants at villages. They have enough to eat, for the first time in the lives. Food and clothes are cheap — and, strange to say, plentifu Cigarettes are terrible, but I'm always hearing they have good on in the next town. (I fear I'll never reach that "next" town.) Th unit entered Madrid defense trenches, University Section, ‹ December 28th, for the heaviest bombardment experienced so fa and the men behaved wonderfully. Thomas Patten from Achi County, Mayo, and Patrick Berry from Northern Ireland wer killed on December 29th. Since then we have eight wounded an one missing.

I am now pressed for time as I have interviews with the Frenc press and making arrangements to speak over the Madrid radio.

I go to school — to the kids of Madrid. They get a great kick ou of my Spanish, and always I'm reminded of that bundle of mischi of yours back in Dublin — and I get lonesome.

I will write you soon again, in the meantime, send me all the nev and remember me to all the crowd. Good luck.

FRANK

Socoro Rojo, Hospital de Sangre, Elda, February 17, 1937
Dear Helen & Gerald:

The above address should be enough to let you know that I ar off the Active List for a little while. I got a bullet through the le: arm a few days ago, on the South Madrid front. It's not serious an I'm not confined to bed. I count myself lucky: it was the fourth da of a pretty tough fight, and anyway, I have escaped for a long tim‹ haven't I? As I went out on a stretcher I heard the Yanks come i — so expect news from them soon.

I got five letters from you — mostly together — after I cam back at the end of January from Madrid. I got Helen's letter enclos ing that *brilliant* "New York Post" cutting about myself just as was going up the line. I guess I'll pick up more news in a day or tw‹ I'm here in a sunny climate, where there are actually baths an barbers — so I'm not too badly off.

Why can't I write oftener? Well, I certainly could have written postcards — but probably I wasn't in the humor. I'm sorry to have to refuse to write those newspaper articles: I have had similar requests from London and Dublin — but the censorship here is sensible: you go up the line as a soldier, or you stay behind as a correspondent. And if you stay behind, what can you write of? I guess I could get special permission, if I tried, but then I'd have to omit mention of places, dates and units — so it wouldn't be worth the trouble. And anyway, what did I come out here for? To be another O'Duffy, directing his men from the rear — would you like me that way? Would I like myself?

Which reminds me — why must the "Post" and other papers talk of this "bloodfeud" between O'Duffy and I? We would be out here, if there never was an O'Duffy. We smashed his attempts to set up his dictatorship in Ireland — and, as *you* know, he came here to find the career that he could not get in Ireland. We came here to fight fascism; it's just an accident for us that O'Duffy happens to be here fighting for it. And, the pity is that the vast majority of those whom he enticed into Franco's camp are just fools who think they are "Fighting for the Faith." I've seen how Franco and his German and Italian masters "Fight for the Faith." The bodies of babies cluttered in a schoolyard after an air-raid, breadlines of women blown to bits, workingclass houses razed. And you heard of the Bull-Rings of Badajoz and other towns which the fascists took? And the women who are turned over — one to every twenty Moors? That's the kind of Faith *they* fight for, it . . . well — to Hell with it!

I'll write you in a few days. I've lost some of my best, including Kit Conway who led No. 1 Company since the start. Another boy is with the Americans and I await news. Regards to all the crowd.

FRANK

Spain, February 11, 1937

Dear Gerald:

I've had some days' rest (during which I didn't write you!) and I'm feeling fit now. I'm pretty well acclimatized. I can even roll a cigarette (of the world's worst tobacco) and my throat stands up to

115

From Spanish Trenches

it. I lost my voice for a week, when I first came, but now I keep fre
from colds. The days, as a rule, are brilliantly sunny; it freezes a
night. Rain is rare — but even so — the roads are like those o
Flanders. And you can't believe what Spanish lorry-drivers wi
chance, until you come here. I tell you I'm more afraid of them tha
I am of aeroplanes or even machine-guns.

Not one of my boys let me down. Every man justified his selec
tion. And when this war is over, I'll be able to tell just what the
did, and the difficulties under which they did it. Kids some of ther
were — lads not nineteen years old, who told me they were twenty
four — and they were heroes. Down in Andalusia, someone sprea
the story that O'Duffy's men were opposite us. When the order t
go over came, you should have seen our lads charge. "Up the Re
public!" "To hell with the fascists!" — the old war cries rang out al
along the line. (Of course, O'Duffy and his men were doing polic
work in Salamanca that day.) One incident of that fight is typical
Jack Nalty of Dublin was caught in machine gun fire. He has thre
bullets in his chest and his right arm broke. He picked up his rifl
and slung it over the good shoulder, caught up the broken arm, an
walked three kilometers to the field hospital. "Others need stretch
ers more," he said. Of course, a man with such an iron constitutio
is alive and on the mend today.

Who'd think that a sensitive chap like Frank Edwards coul
stand up to this kind of war? Yet, none better than he.

Paris, March 5, 1937

Gerald, rooting in my haversack today, I found the foregoing —
a letter I was beginning to write you in the village called Chincon
south of Madrid, when the order came to go up the line. We wer
in action at dawn the next day on the Jarama front. (That's wher
Franco had driven a wedge in south of Madrid, menacing the only
road out, i.e., that to Valencia.) I had been previously in Universit
City, in Caso de Campo, and in Guadarrama — I guess it's almos
time to tell you that I have been in the firing line continuousl
from four days after my arrival in Spain — but Jarama was th
toughest fighting I ever saw; artillery, while pretty accurate o
both sides, is not intensive in Spain; three or four field-pieces to a

116

attalion is the custom. But the machine-gun fire was terrific, and hen there were mortars, tanks and aeroplanes. Old Great War soldiers tell me the machine-gun fire was more intensive than in 1914–18. We were fighting German and Italian regulars. They were dressed in corduroy uniforms, but they weren't Spaniards, nor Moors. In one machine-gun nest a group of us wiped out, I picked four German passports out of the pockets of the crew. I saw letters and papers in Italian taken from dead fascist infantry the same day. I must admit these fascists were good fighters and were well officered. They were obviously picked troops, for the sector is the key to Madrid. If the fascists succeeded there, Madrid was isolated. Need I tell you our casualties were terrific? Most of the Irish were in the No. 1 Company, of the English speaking Battalion, but there were others in the other companies too. The Batt. Adj. was Irish, and I was on the Batt. Staff as Polit. Commissar. Our No. 1 Company, as usual, got the toughest job — leading the attack. After the first day's fighting it was reduced from one hundred and forty three to fifty eight. The O/C — "Kit" Conway of Dublin, my right-hand man, got three bullets in the groin and died that night. On the second day of the fighting our battalion O/C was wounded. From then on I was (unofficially) in command — and I became a real soldier! Tanks walked through us (it was then that the O/C was wounded) and we were driven back nearly a mile. I marched the battalion back, two hours later, cheered them, cursed them, drove them, led them — and singing the "Internationale" we reoccupied our position. And of them all, there haven't been ten Irishmen left; the rest were killed and wounded.

On the fourth day of the battle (which was continuous — there were occasions when there were only three hundred of us in one line, between the fascists and the Madrid road!) I got a slight flesh-wound in the left arm from a bullet that went through the head of a man beside me. It just made me — even gentle me! — fighting mad. Curious how reckless I got — especially when — as I will tell you later — you realize the circumstances under which I went into that particular battle. Half an hour later, a tank-shell burst beside me and I got a wallop in the left leg that knocked me down. My pantaloons weren't cut, there was no blood. It must have been a stone thrown by the shell. I limped for a few minutes, then I felt

117

From Spanish Trenches

O.K. I then decided we'd dash ahead of the barrage to better posi tions. Shortly after we had done so, I got a bullet through the left arm. It's a clean wound, high up, and will be O.K. in a few weeks more. No bones broken, but a muscle appears to be hurt! And — here's the queer thing — my leg, the left, has been giving me trou ble for the past week, after I had walked without trouble for eight or ten days! In a hospital here, they say (as far as my pidgin French interprets them) that a tendon is wrenched and that I must rest. I'll rest when I get to Dublin.

Which reminds me — the Spanish Government has paid my way back to Ireland, sending me by plane from Valencia to Toulouse (I was afraid to risk air-travel further!!!) "El Commandante Ryan" has their "fullest confidence" and is "a person loyal to the legitimate government" and so goes on a propaganda mission. (They pay only one-way fare. No other expenses.)

Now Gerald, what about a tour of U.S.A.? Would it work? I could arrive in Mid-April — but who would pay expenses? Write to Dublin and let me know.

I'm sorry to be leaving Spain. And I want you and everyone else to understand that if it had so happened that my corpse was now rotting with those others whose stench nearly drove me insane in University City — my life would not have been wasted. Every life given in Spain is another reason why fascism must not pass. If I must take the responsibility for Irish casualties there — my con science is clear, even though parents will not understand it, and even though they will blame me. Our lads who died out there, have not died in vain. They will be an inspiration to us in Ireland when (for I'm afraid there is no "if") our turn comes, and fascism has to be defeated there.

I used to think that my life was worth only one man's life in Spain, and that it was worth half a dozen at home. That was not vanity. I believed, at the time, it was sound political reasoning. I was wrong. My life might be more easily lost in such a terrific war as that in Spain than it would be in Ireland — and that is the only difference between dying in Ireland and dying in Spain. It is merely a difference in degree of longevity. If I died in Spain I would die for human liberty as certainly — perhaps more certainly — than I would in Ireland today.

118

Well — this is a long letter, and I recall that your eyesight isn't too good nor my handwriting too legible — so I'll wind up. I hope you understand now how obstructed I was in Spain and how difficult it was for me to write articles, (even if I got a permit — I wouldn't be in the humor to write the stuff you wanted). What a fool I was that I didn't just bring one or two hundred lads with I.R.A. training out with me. Honestly, Gerald, we'd have wiped out the fascists every time! For efficiency, for courage, and for principle our lads are second to none. I go home full of faith in our people — and more of an Irishman than ever I was.

FRANK

P.S. I had a long interview with Del Vayo (Foreign Minister) last week. He was impressed with my presentation of the case for a Spanish Consul in Dublin and will appoint one shortly.

By the way — the military position in Spain is good, despite all Franco's statements. The *Daily Mail* has reported that English taken prisoners by fascists (some were captured in Jarama, or at least are missing) have signed statements attacking the government. Names of them appended to such statements do not correspond with any members of the English-speaking battalion!

Franco is making his last and biggest push mainly with Germans and Italians. If (as announced today) we are attacking Talavera, that push of Franco's has failed. French frontier is solidly closed against our recruits for past two weeks; and since beginning of year we could get only driblets out from England and Ireland. Yet Franco has now till March 30th to get more men in.

February 5, 1937

Dear Friends:

I read in the *Irish Press* that "the Wild Geese have flown again;" I read in the *Irish Echo,* New York, of the "tragedy" of men like me coming out here. The type of canned nationalism that inspires such talk is THE tragedy I deplore. They ignore the changes in world politics, they would have us ignore the Great Danger until it is on our shores. "We serve Ireland only," they cry, but they would have

119

us wait until it would be too late to make effective use of our services. Catalonia recognises that it must not wait until Franco reaches its borders. Is Ireland to commit the error Catalonia avoids?

Is the *Irish Press* comparing the Wild Geese to O'Duffy's hirelings? The Wild Geese were honest-minded men who went out to fight against their country's enemy. (Incidentally, their fate should have forever killed the slogan: "England's enemy is Ireland's friend.") To compare O'Duffy's dupes with them is an insult to national tradition. Does O'Duffy go to fight against even "England's enemy?"

What mistakes — yes, tragedies — are caused by failing to face facts. Not ten percent of O'Duffy's forces in Spain are fascists; the rest of them are just dupes who go to "fight for the Faith." The *Irish Press* refused to say that, for it fears to tackle the pro-Fascist Irish Hierarchy, yet to avoid alienating Republican opinion, it has to shadow-box with O'Duffy. And there is no paper to champion truth and justice unequivocally. How can we let the world know that the lives of Conroy and Coady, Meehan and Boyle, have not been wasted, that their deaths are not "tragedies" that need not have happened? Honor to those who died for the freedom of the Irish people; honor even greater to those who die here for the freedom of ALL HUMANITY. No "Wild Geese" were these lads. You remember how I warned them, before they left home, what their life here — as long as it would last — would be like. You remember how I discouraged every suspicion of adventurism. You know how they could have stayed at home and be regarded by their friends as "soldiers of Ireland." They chose to come here asking neither for pay nor preferment, coming because they believed it was their duty to come to participate in this decisive fight against Fascism. And, for my part, while it would be wrong to accuse me of bringing them here, I would never regret having done so. Our 50,000 who died in the Great War were sacrificed uselessly; no life given here is given in vain.

And look at it from the purely selfish viewpoint. Which is better: that some of us should die here, or that thousands should die at home? For if Fascism triumphs here, Ireland's trial will soon be at hand.

FRANK RYAN

120

Ireland

JOE MONKS, an I.R.A. man, was commanding officer of the 4th Battalion in the Dublin Brigade.

January 15, 1937

Dear Uncle:

I'm in hospital here with an in-and-out hole through the flesh of the chest. I got it when the Irish section and the other English-speaking company were ordered to clear up an enemy position which was holding up our left flank. We were brought to the front in lorries.

I was among those to reach the line in the first lorry. We lay down in a field awaiting the rest of the company. An airplane saw us and down it swooped, giving us a rattle of machine gun fire. To tell the truth I buried my face into the earth and waited for the bang, but it passed on without harming us. Our Captain called us out on the road; there we met the rest, beginning the advance. I was meeting my pals with a grin, but I lost it quickly when young Fox told me that the plane had killed Negal, a Londoner, who had joined us.

However, the advance went on up a sand road. Then the machine guns opened up and we continued through an olive grove. A French Unit was holding a position in front of us. We were swinging to the left, leaving the olive grove, and began to climb a bare ridge. There was a bomber overhead. It was not dropping bombs; it was directing the enemy machine guns, and they were giving us the works. We passed over the ridge in short rushes and up the next one. It was then we sighted the enemy advancing. We then gained it and poured our fire into a villa which was the enemy's key position. It was here that I got hit. An English lad and a chap from Glasgow brought me to a dressing station; from there a Frenchman brought me to the road where I was picked up by an ambulance.

In the hospital we are treated like lords. We get all sorts of good things; during visiting hours the whole town passes through the wards, and the poor people give us everything they have. My pals and I are thinking of starting a fruit shop we have got so much. Of course there are orange trees growing along the streets.

All over Spain and Southern France, the people give you the

Popular Front salute, and the kiddies sing the Internationale as they play in the streets. It was played as we marched through Barcelona, with Frank Ryan carrying our banner.

We have great artillery, French 75 guns. The Government representative in this town can speak English; he has invited me to stay and take a job when the war is over.

I hope all of you are "game-ball."

JOE

Hospital de Sangre, Orihucea, February 5, 1937

Dear Aunt:

When I was in hospital at Linares members of the Student Association came every day to see the wounded, and, making the best of my bit of Latin, I became very friendly with them and when I was able to move around they brought me to their homes where we spent the afternoon sitting around a brazier of charcoal and talking the best we could. They made it clear to me that they were not anti-God, but as they say in Spanish *"anti-fascist y anti-cura."* Most of them proclaim themselves Catholics and expect to be able to practice their religion when the war is over. They all seemed pleased that the old oppression is smashed; even the nuns in the hospital showed no malice towards us.

Franco is doing his damndest to break down the resistance of the people, but he can't succeed. Up to now the odds were all on his side; his airplanes ruled the air and all the modern war weapons of Germany and Italy were mowing down the legions of Militia, but the courage of the Spanish and the wonderful role of the International Brigade held up his progress until the workers had time to shape themselves into soldiers.

There is one thing I want to tell you, that is if the I.R.A. and Fianna Fail follow the policy of Pontius Pilate and give Fascism a chance to make a bid for power in Ireland, if even a hundred men raise the flag of the people and if they defend the remotest mountain for a length of time, the Column will rush to their assistance.

Perhaps it is just because I am a member of the Column that I think such a lot about it, but you will know that my description of it is not just boast. In the short time I have been in Spain I have

122

made many friends and met many great men. I will do my best to give you an impression of life in Spain at present. In every town behind the Government lines there are thousands of men in the uniform of the Republic and among them stride the wounded of the Brigade, admired by all.

The Brigade is truly international. You find men from the four corners of the earth, but the French are the best. Nobody equals them on their advance. Germans hold a line well. The Germans are fugitives from Hitler's terror and are fighting for a refuge to live in, while the French will return to their own country. In the stores, in the Red Cross and in the front lines the French are in the majority. Their 75's are the best guns for this kind of war and they are always used to great effect.

As yet I have not witnessed any member of the Brigade break any of the laws of the community. There is no doubt that the cream of the world's working class is in Spain; they would go to the red hob of hell to fight Fascism.

I may have mentioned that the French machine gunners under Captain Alexandra made a great name for themselves in the action in which I took part. Did you know Ralph Fox, the English author? He was killed in the same fight that morning. He had explained the position of the enemy and the nature of the ground to me as we sat on the side of the road waiting to move off.

After we have won in Spain, we will come back to Ireland.

JOE

↔

BILL SCOTT refers to the return of the Christian Fronters to Ireland in this letter. These troops were brought to Spain by the fascist O'Duffy under the pretext that they would defend the Church in another holy crusade.

February 27, 1937

Dear Sean:

I am writing this letter in a hurry and under sad circumstances. Kit's name has been added to the Roll of Honor. With him on the Southern Front of Madrid fell Mick Nolan and the Coy.

From Spanish Trenches

Adjt., Paddy McDaid, veteran of the Four Courts in 1922, Frank Ryan and Jim Prendergast were wounded in the same engagement Frank is doing well. I was with him all night on Thursday and saw him away on Friday morning. Sean, you know what Kit was to me. You, at least, will understand how I feel now. I can hardly write this letter. But Kit has only gone on before us. He made many silent sacrifices in the cause of the poor and oppressed of our country; in the end he gave his life. He could give no more than that. Kit was a great soldier, and a lover of justice. Though his familiar smile will never again comfort us in our struggles, his memory must inspire us. To turn back now would be treachery to Kit. Over Kit's grave, and over the graves of all our comrades, we swear: "They Shall Not Pass!"

Frank's spirit is unbreakable. When I asked: "Is it true, Frank?" he did not speak, but the look in his face said "yes, it is true." When Frank broke the silence, he said: "Bill, we must never let Kit down; we must fight it to a finish." We know Frank Ryan well enough to know he will not break his promise. He has been at the head of his men in the thick of the fight. He would be with the rest of the glorious Irish Column today were his arm not in a sling. He has lost his best lieutenant, he has seen his Column getting smaller every day, he has seen the grim determination of his small, but gallant band of heroes to carry on to the end. They know Frank will never let them down; they would follow him to hell with rifles on their shoulders. He is determined to carry the flag of the Irish Column to victory or death. He is now in the South recovering from his wound.

The town where I am now was heavily bombed last night. The bombers were accompanied by fighting planes which machine-gunned the unfortunate women running for shelter. The central pharmacy, a big building used for storing medical appliances and equipment, bandages, etc., and for housing doctors was the first building to be bombed. It was blown to pieces and a number of ambulances wrecked. This made the rescue work more difficult. Whether this was deliberate or accidental I leave to your judgment, but my experience of naked Fascism and what it can do, makes me believe anything.

I hear the "Christian Fronters" want to get back from Spain. I predicted that months ago. What a contrast between their letters

124

and those sent from our side of the frontier. Men here have sworn not to stop till Spain is free from Fascist murder or till death stops them. Give my regards to all the comrades. On with the fight on the home front. Victory will soon be ours — for Fascism is digging its grave in Spain.

BILL

↔

FATHER RAMON DE LABORDA is a Basque priest who is now living in Ireland. He was attacked by an Irish priest because of his loyalty to the cause of the rightful Spanish government. Since Father Gannon, the Irish priest who comes to the defense of Franco's insurgents, has not been in Spain, I feel that his letters have no place in these pages. Father Laborda's answers, which appeared in the Irish Press of Dublin, a paper which does not enjoy the reputation of being a liberal newspaper, deal with Father Gannon's attack with all the fairness that one could expect from one who has consecrated his life to God.

"Kingston" Dundrum Co. Dublin, January 15, 1937

Dear Sir,

Father Gannon will permit me to keep clearly before the Irish people in this controversy that I am here to explain that the Civil War in Spain is not a religious war, but that Catholics fight on both sides, just as there are atheists on both sides. I have no mission but to state the facts. When they are known the Irish people will make their decision, and beyond that I do not presume to go.

It will help for a proper understanding of events if people will remember that in the anti-fascist part of the Basque country, where there exists that alliance between Popular Front and Basque Nationalists which so horrifies Franco's friends, that our churches are crowded as they always were, and that soldiers fighting Franco attend there and receive the Sacraments, that priests go up to the firing line and comfort the soldiers, praying with them when they are wounded and praying over their graves when they go to rest. Father Gannon will find it hard to convince a Catholic people that the Bishop of Vitoria in whose diocese this takes place can be as hostile as he would make out, when all this work by his priests has his lordship's wholehearted Blessing.

125

From Spanish Trenches

I should like to say, too, that a fortnight before the outbreak of the Civil War I was in Madrid where I moved around freely in my clerical garb and received only courtesy and friendliness. The Basque representatives in the Spanish Parliament attended my Mass and President Aguirre was the first to receive the Blessed Eucharist from my fingers that day. And Father Gannon asks the Irish people to believe that such a man is an instrument of anti-religious fury.

It is true that there were attacks on Churches in the interval between the February elections and the July rising. In these months conditions in Spain were very excited for in many places the peasants broke free from their squalor and forcibly seized the large estates, the most outstanding example being at Badajoz, where later such fearful vengeance was exacted by the Fascists. Calvo Sotelo and the others, inciting the outrages against Churches, took pains to conceal the fact that these outrages took place where priests became the centre of the resistance to the peasant risings, and Father Gannon, who can so easily understand what Fascist officers do to priests who oppose them, will understand how easily these oppressed peasants turned to their outrages. I think it is monstrous to make men believe they are attacking the Cross when they attack the fences of the grandees, in such circumstances as those obtaining in many parts of Spain. It was not to defend the Churches but to defend their estates that the officers in the army rose in revolt.

And now for a few outstanding differences between Father Gannon and me. He very graciously withdraws any suggestion that it was I who said the revered Bishop of Vitoria yielded to a pistol. And he further obliges me by reading the two recent letters received at the Jesuit House, Milltown Park, from the Bishop of Vitoria. These letters are not so secret as he would seem to think, and, indeed, he reveals their contents to some extent himself for he says they make no mention of any duress in the signing of the pastoral issued in association with the Bishop of Pamplona. I will draw on these letters, too, and quote briefly:

"I lament all the horrors that have fallen on my poor country. I, myself am a victim of this unjust and terrible oppression . . . My priests are very good and they suffer *unjust* persecution."

126

But Fr. Gannon may have heard also of the rumour so freely circulated in the Basque country and of which Mr. Martin gave a version. Here are some facts about the pastoral, and Fr. Gannon can easily communicate them himself to my beloved bishop, whose address they have at Milltown Park:

1 — The pastoral was not written either by the Bishop of Vitoria or the Bishop of Pamplona who signed it, but by the Cardinal Archbishop of Toledo.

2 — That before signing the pastoral the bishop of Vitoria wished to put in an addendum to tell his children on both sides that he sent them his blessing but was not permitted to do so.

3 — If it is not true that His Lordship was forced to quit San Sebastian because of his protests against Fascist outrages.

Father Gannon in conclusion contrasts our attitude in holding open Irun for arms from abroad with the defence of Pamplona with St. Ignatius; may I point out in passing that Ignatius the soldier had little in common with Ignatius the saint, whose saintliness began when he laid down the sword after being wounded at Pamplona. But on this matter of the crime of receiving foreign arms, I should like to put Father Gannon a question:

In 1922 there was Civil War in Ireland. One side got arms freely from England and the other side was blockaded. The Irish Bishops were as vehemently on one side as the published pastorals would put the Bishops in Spain. If the forces under President de Valera had got arms from Russia and won the war, does Father Gannon think that the Catholic Church would have been destroyed in Ireland as a consequence? In answering that question he will answer the question Basque Nationalists ask themselves in seeking their freedom in association with Left forces in Spain and outside it,

I am, dear sir,

Yours faithfully,

(Rev.) RAMON DE LABORDA

"Kingston," Dundrum, Co. Dublin

A Letter from Guernica

*HENRY HART is an American author and newspaper correspond-
ent who was born in staid Philadelphia — in the shadow of Liberty
Bell — in 1903. For several years he was an editor of the publishing
house of G. P. Putnam & Sons. Among his published works is
a novel, "The Great One." He also edited a volume about the first
Writers Congress ever held in the United States, "American Writers
Congress."*

Guernica, Spain, February 20, 1937

Dear Marcel:

. You asked me to write at least once and tell you what it is
actually like here in the Basque country now that all Spain is
in the turmoil of war. How often on the boat coming over I wondered what it would be like. In the United States there are only
a few people, all over eighty, who remember what civil war is
like.

In Bilbao, where we are staying, the war is a reality every minute of the day. The population has doubled and the streets are
swollen with refugees. Sandbags are piled against the windows
and everywhere there are signs — "refugio" — telling the
people where to seek shelter when next the German planes are
overhead.

But here in this lovely little village of Guernica — we would call
it a village at home although it has five or six thousand people — I
have no awareness of war. I cannot believe, as I sit in the window of
this little hotel, that only twenty miles away is the battle line I
visited yesterday, or that shells are falling in Madrid, or that
Málaga is in ruins and seven thousand men, women and children,
fleeing from that unhappy city, have just been massacred from the
air.

No, I have difficulty, here in this little country town, lying amid
these gray and green Basque mountains, in believing there is a war.
It is true that my eye cannot find any young men, but save for this,

128

there is no sign of war. The señora who keeps this hotel talked at lunch about spring, whether it is really here, whether it is safe to plant, or whether a frost will come and destroy what was planted too soon. Yes, now that I recall a certain strain in her voice, I can see that her's is no ordinary concern. There is not much food, and an early spring will help. So perhaps I am shutting my eyes, as one does when one has been too long amid pain.

And yet this morning, when I visited the building which, a hundred years ago, housed the Basque parliament; when I saw the carefully preserved trunk of the great oak under which, many hundreds of years ago, the Basque parliament met and under which the Spanish kings swore to respect the *fueros* (the separate and democratic laws of the Basques); and when the librarian unlocked the vault and showed me the book of the Basque constitution, hand-illumined in 1342, and told me one of the sentences of our constitution is from that ancient code — it was as though the scholarly librarian and I were immersed in the remote past before Columbus set out on his voyage.

But I see now that once again there was an undertone, for when the librarian asked me to write a few words in the guest book, as he hospitably asks all who visit here to do, I wrote without thinking, and as a matter of course, "May Euskadi (the Basque race) always fight fascism." And when I translated this, the librarian nodded and accepted it as a matter of course. And so you can see that though the serenity of this little town seems untroubled, there is underneath, in all of the people, the recognition that a modern scourge is abroad and that it must be vanquished.

Yes, this is the most important thing that I have found in Spain. The heroic Spanish people have already won victories which the entire German and Italian armies combined can never obliterate from life.

The first and foremost of these victories is the disproof of the fiction cherished by the timid in the middle classes and the hypocrites in owning classes of all countries, to the effect that communism is the instigator of violence, the prime mover against democracy.

I don't think the international capitalists realize that by fomenting this fascist revolt in Spain they have undone years of costly (to themselves) work. The simple, trusting man-of-the-street knows now — so definitely and realistically that no dissuasion, threats or trickery can confuse him — that it is *fascism*, not communism, which resorts to armed violence when a democracy at last votes in a government that is actually devoted to a better life for *all*.

The doubting Thomases among our own intellectuals don't realize the extent of this victory. They need no longer concern themselves with the search for a euphemistic synonym for communism. The so-called onus, which capitalistic propaganda put on the word communism, has been dissolved for millions of men and women all over the world in the holocaust loosed by the fascists upon Spain.

The word communism and the idea of it as a way of life no longer quicken the blind prejudice and hate which capitalists have worked so hard to engender. I found this to be true even on the boat going to Europe. The American wife, aged thirty-five, of a French Senator (Radical Socialist, aged seventy) assured a German baron who was a friend of Fritz Thyssen that communism (which she did not want) was going to triumph, and an English lord, a member of the Labor Party, confessed that Spain had shown him that the next step for him was not anarchism — for which, he said, he had always had a kind of suppressed desire — but communism. And in France even the gendarmes know what communism is. I mean what it really is. I asked one of them where Thorez was speaking. Instead of looking blank and saying "Who?", or arresting me (which would certainly have happened in Jersey City), he said he didn't know but that the gendarme on the other corner knew a café proprietor who knew Thorez and that he could find out. He did so and came back with the information.

Here in Spain people who, in normal times, would be highly reactionary, speak of communists as men of courage, worthy of the greatest admiration. Catholics speak of the communists fighting with them as of friends whose views differ only in a few minor particulars from their own. Three Catholic priests, at different times, have told me that they not only personally prefer communism to fascism but that they are convinced the Church itself would ultimately find that it must do so too.

130

The U.S.A.

This is a profound change. It extends, or will extend, into every country and corner of the world. It can never be undone.

The second great victory already won in Spain is the substitution of rationality for mass delusions of all kinds. The importance of this second victory is manifest when it is remembered with what glee and loving care capitalism nurtures and cultivates irrational ideas, surcharging them with emotion so that they become passionate beliefs and the perfect dividers of man from man.

This is especially visible in this part of Spain. Here Basque nationalism is the dominant political factor, but you find all parties — Basque Nationalism, Catholicism, Anti-Clericalism, Free Masonry, Republicanism, Centrism, Federalism, Monarchism, Carlism, Socialism, Communism and Anarchism. Men believe in all these things, but they no longer hate those who believe in something different from themselves, *for one idea now pervades them all.* They are all fighting for one thing, the defeat of Franco, and they all know now that at bottom one thing is *their* enemy, and the enemy of progress, and that all of them have to do something to get rid of it. And this one thing is the profit system.

This is true throughout Spain, and the parties of the left have carried this second victory of the Spanish victory to the necessary, inevitable conclusion — unification on the *way* to get rid of Franco and the profit system he fights for. This is so true that the Socialist and Communist parties in Catalonia have already united, and these two parties will probably merge here in the Basque country in the very near future. It is so true that in an Anarchist paper which I picked up in Santander the leading editorial exhorted the Anarchists to develop with all speed a *discipline similar to that of the Communist Party.*

The eradication from the face of the world of antithetical beliefs, of old superstitions left over from previous historical epochs, obsolete customs and mores, provincialisms, localisms, and individualisms, all of which have separated man from man, and in man's struggle toward freedom have confused him, weakened him and defeated him — this eradication has been accomplished not only in Spain, but, because of the events in Spain, has been accelerated throughout the world.

The world importance of this simplification of human thought lies in this: the imminent attainment of world unity — in thought and action. World unity is really the goal of human evolution, and certainly of social and political evolution. And the tempo of its attainment has been quickened throughout the world by the pragmatic effects of the events in Spain. When future generations look back upon our time and read of our struggles to release ourselves from the bondage that has always enslaved and degraded us, this unification of thought will be deemed of greater historical importance than the conquest of fire, the discovery of the wheel, the Copernican theory — all of which will be reduced to their rightful proportion, i.e., steps on the way to making the whole world kin.

Here indeed is the regimentation of which capitalist intellectuals complain, and the reason why they do so. Here is the unified power of the entire human race ridding itself for all time of ignorance, superstition and emotional nonsense, ridding itself of all the intellectual chains which have made it possible for capitalism to survive, freeing itself for new intellectual exploration and discovery, for new insight into the universe, into the physiology of our bodies, into the psychology of our minds, into the potentialities of our mental and physical energies for transforming the world.

The third great victory of Spanish heroism is the world-wide intensification of militant anti-fascism. In Spain men and women are determined to die rather than surrender. They *have* died, and each death has bred an anti-fascist — a friend, a mother, a wife, a relative of someone who has died. When one sees one's babies bombed, one's husband's body defiled, one's country invaded by foreign mercenary troops — nothing can *ever* extirpate the resistance to fascism and the determination to vanquish it. That is why there cannot possibly be a fascist victory in Spain. Too much blood has been given, too many homes have been destroyed, too many cities have been laid waste.

One afternoon, behind the loyalist lines on the front near San Sebastian, a young Basque of twenty showed me a letter from his fiancée. "Although all my desire and all my hopes are bound to you," she wrote, "I would rather you were killed than that we should live on as slaves to the fascists." On the same front, last summer, just after the fascists began the devastation of Spain, men went against machine guns *with bare hands*. "And we'll do it

132

gain," said one of them. As I looked from face to face the heads of
is companions one by one nodded assent.

And so in all countries. In France, for example, where the determination of the French people against war was the cement which
originally bound the Front Populaire, the determination which now
binds all political parties except those of the right is that there shall
be no fascism, not in France, nor in Belgium, nor Czechoslovakia —
and not in Germany nor Italy nor Japan.

These victories, which the heroic Spanish people have already
given to the world, tower above the military news from day to day.
They are permanent victories; no counter attack will ever destroy
them. Here, in the extreme north of Spain, the Loyalists hold a
narrow strip of mountainous land two hundred miles long. Between
the sea and Franco's line there are sometimes ten, never more than
thirty miles. For eight months this small strip of land has been
inviolate. "We will never be conquered," one of the Basque officials
said to me yesterday, "for before we could be conquered we will all
be dead."

No one can come into the midst of such valor and be the same
person he was before he entered it. No one can be present in its
midst without a profound and complete belief in the final victory.
When the history of our times is written, Marcel, it will be seen that
we were living through a renaissance greater than the one which
woke the world from its long mediaeval sleep, and it will then be
seen that the tide turned toward the future in Spain in the year
1937.

I do hope, Marcel, that you and all our friends will make the
cause of the Spanish people your own. In that way we will be on the
side of *life*. I look forward to joining you in this work when I get
back.

Sincerely,

HENRY

The Abraham Lincoln Battalion

In the front lines of the Spanish war there can be found a group of boys and men who live cheerfully and die bravely, and who, in the overalls that are the uniform of those who fight for the Spanish Republic, are readily recognized as boys from home: "Yankees." They come from every walk of life: among them there are steelworkers and artists, furriers and school teachers. Their battalion carries the name of Abraham Lincoln. To them he was the man from the ranks of the people who lived for freedom and who died for it. And if they never learn to speak another word of Spanish, you may be sure they know what they mean when they yell in unison: "NO PASARAN."

Herbert L. Matthews is the Madrid correspondent of The New York Times. His article of April 25, 1937 is reprinted here as an introduction to the letters that follow.

London, April 22, 1937

In December some 450 American youngsters with a sprinkling of older men who had seen service in the World War arrived in Spain to fight with the Loyalists under the designation "Lincoln Battalion." Today fewer than a third are alive and unscathed.

The Americans had health, zeal and courage, but they knew nothing of soldiering and had precious little time to learn it in.

The Spanish conflict is a poor man's war. There were no soldiers or material to spare and those were critical days when it appeared that Madrid might be encircled.

Besides, the Americans were impatient to get into the fray and do their part in what they considered to be a crusade against fascism. They had some intensive training at a town near Albacete, where most of them learned to shoot rifles and the rest to handle machine guns, which is all that the true internationalists are doing on the Loyalist side.

Then came that dangerous push against the Valencia road the middle of January. The Insurgents broke through along the Jarama

River and pushed to within 500 yards of the highway before mixed brigades stopped them and drove them back a little.

But worse was to come for the Rebels struck again, this time at a tangent up the Tajuna Valley toward Morata, and there the fiercest and bloodiest struggle of the civil war took place. Every available mixed brigade with its international troops was rushed into line.

In a sense it was a decisive struggle, for to have lost that battle might well have sealed the doom of Madrid. There was no time to hesitate, no time to spare any man who could be thrown in.

The Americans were still raw as soldiers, but they were ripe in spirit and the Lincoln Battalion was rushed up to join the English battalion of the Fifteenth mixed brigade, with whom they received their baptism of fire a few miles southwest of Morata.

That was a retreating action whose object was to retard the Rebels until a strong stand could be made a short distance back. The Americans were fighting in open terrain under exceptionally heavy fire, but they took it well and showed their officers that they were to be relied upon.

In subsequent days, when the mixed brigades held firm and General Francisco Franco's forces beat against an impregnable defense, the Americans were still in that front line.

The Morata sector is composed of a mass of rather sharp hills — easy to defend and suicidal to attack for every inch of it can be covered by machine-gun cross-fire.

The fighting developed into a deadlock. Those of us who were going down to Morata to cover the battle could sense the growing confidence and strengthened morale of the troops as it became apparent that General Franco's forces would not pass.

The American headquarters was in a little house not far from the main square of the village, and it was like a corner of home to us newspaper men. There was even a grinning Negro from down South to greet us as we walked in; there were good fellowship and excellent meals.

The battalion had not yet suffered heavy casualties. Perhaps as many as 400 of the original 450 were left.

Then it was decided to launch an attack from the government side. The strategists no doubt knew their business. They wanted to take Pingarron Hill, which dominated the terrain southwest of

From Spanish Trenches

Morata. The fifteenth Brigade held that sector, and it was the
who received orders to take the hill.

The tactics were the normal ones — an artillery barrage, a tan
charge and then the men swept forward. They went into a fearfu
machine-gun barrage, but they kept going. They even stumble
upward until the hill was almost theirs.

Yet it was a hopeless charge, repeated vainly during that day an
part of the next. When it was over Pingarron Hill remained In
surgent and of the 400 Americans in the Lincoln Battalion, 10
were left. Of course the casualties included wounded in addition t
dead.

Already thirty or thirty-five wounded have returned to the bat
talion. More Americans — we do not know how many, but the bat
talion hoped there would be enough to refill the ranks — are i
training now and will soon be fighting.

The Jarama River front has been relatively quiet, but the nee
for men is too great for any to be spared and a week ago at least th
Americans were still there. They have had a terrible baptism of fire
but their spirit remains high, as one recent incident showed.

Typhoid broke out in that sector and it became necessary t
inoculate all the troops. A few internationals tried to refuse, but th
Americans took it without a murmur and moreover took it in the
front line trenches.

Needless to say, the presence or absence of 400 men is not going
to make a great amount of difference in the civil war and there is no
need to exaggerate the military importance of the Lincoln Battalion
But the important thing is that they are typical of thousands of
others who are doing what they are doing, and that has made a
great difference.

HERBERT L. MATTHEWS

136

The U.S.A.

PAUL BURNS is a native of New York State. He graduated from Middlebury College in Vermont and taught school for several years. He has also written for a number of periodicals and was reporter and columnist on Our World, a Boston labor paper.

Dear Betsey:

I received two letters and one containing news clippings from you and was mighty mighty glad to get them. Thanks very much.

Eddie and I read the clippings with great interest. Charlie was not here to read them with us as he has been wounded. He is in a hospital and is getting along swell. His wound was in the arm, nasty but not dangerous.

You may have read Ralph Bates' book, *The Olive Field*, — I have not read it but it deals with the situation in Spain. I am reminded of the title because there are thousands of olive trees here. The unpicked olives age on the trees and drop to the ground, literally covering it. The juice is a wine-like purple when the olives rot. In the past we have learned lots about olives from the most intimate association, lying among them on the ground until we were all over purple-red color. It sort of makes you feel something like a salad. I will never see olives again without recalling how they squashed against us as we wriggled our way through the olive fields.

Speaking of trees, sometimes they bear strange fruit. Fascist snipers have a nasty habit of nesting in a tree and popping at one. Or, to re-phrase Mr. Joyce Kilmer's little poem —

> "A tree that may in summer wear
> A nest of maxims in her hair."

A pretty thought. Tsk, tsk.

Phil and Buddy keep wanting to come over. I do not think Phil should, what with a wife and child, nor Buddy, since he has a mother to support.

Mike the maaad man is in Spain. I have not seen him yet. By this time my moustache and red Van Dyke beard should make him feel definitely inferior.

Well, have an applejack sour (just one) for me. Give my regards to everyone and keep an eye out for me.

PAUL

137

From Spanish Trenches

March 23, 1937

Dear Phil:

I am completely recovered and hope you are the same. I hope you and all the gang are well.

Please tell Paul we met Frank Ryan and Frank Edwards here. I met Edwards, Irish Republican leader, in the hospital where he was completely recovered from a bad wound. Tell O'Connor Edwards lived for a while on the Great Blasket. Also please give him my address. Tell him to let us know how the Irish are in Boston.

Charlie, Eddie and I share the same dugout. Frank was also wounded and we expect him to rejoin us in the line any day now.

The war goes on with success on our side. The O'Flaherty's and Paul (now correctly known as the tall thin man) have the situation well in hand. After the war is won we will gladly supply you with fascist helmets which you can use for flower pots and an armoured tank or so to use when collecting dues or transporting MacCallum's Scotch Whiskey.

Put in your order now! Keep a fascist in your back yard instead of a garbage pail! They are guaranteed to be docile and will eat anything. It's the truth. Gen. Franco is not feeding his men very well.

I am going to have one stuffed and mounted later on. It will make an ideal place to put old razor blades in.

Speaking of razors we are all growing beards. I have a long red moustache which would shame even Mike — and in addition a red Van Dyke. Regards —

PAUL

The three O'Flaherty's are Irishmen from Boston, Mass. To them the fight for freedom in Spain was just as important as the battle which has been waged for freedom by the Irish people. Following are letters from two of the brothers.

March 20, 1937

Dear Phil:

Here lads — under adverse circumstances we jot down as much news as we can. We've been at the front now for some time. The Lincoln Battalion has done itself proud on the field of action. Of one

ction a high Spanish officer remarked, "That is one of the most
eroic actions I have ever seen."

Ach, the weather has been cold . . . And the rain continually
alling. It certainly must be breaking down the morale of the fasists. They can't stand this much longer. As a matter of fact, hardly
a night passes but some of them desert to our lines.

There's an Irish section in the Lincoln Battalion, you know. It's
alled the James Connolly section, Paul, Frank, Eddie and I are
n it. With us are some swell fighting men from the old country,
most of whom are I.R.A. men.

Ed was the commander of this body of men until a week ago.
Now he is a company commander. A little over a week ago Eddie,
with Paul and a handful of others from the Irish section, a few
Americans and some Spanish comrades completed an action which
if it had not been done — and done with such quick thinking
bravery — the forces of democracy would have suffered a severe
blow.

And now a short resume of the activities of some of the boys from
New England. Paul got a flesh wound in the arm. He is now back
with us — fit as a fiddle and slender as a chorus girl. He has been
elected political leader of the Irish section.

Frank also was wounded a little later — two in the leg and one in
the arm. All flesh wounds — none serious. We expect to have him
back with us shortly. Before he left for the hospital he was the political leader of a company as well as the first assistant to a company
commander. Now, we are told, he's the life of the party in the hospital. Bob Taylor was also an assistant company commander before
he was hurt. He'll be all right in a short while, too. Tell Grace not to
worry. Bailey was also hurt. He's recovering.

Now don't you guys boast too much. The boys from Boston
aren't the only soldiers leading the government forces to victory.
However, I know Phil will be proud as hell — positively insuffer-
able. Tell him to take it easy. He ain't heard nothing yet. Wait till
the warm weather comes and I thaw out . . . With my bare hands
I'll . . .! Well — never mind . . . You'll read about it in the
papers. I'm political commissar for my company at present.

Some letters sent to us must have been lost in transit. Buddy's
letter was the first we got. We thank him mucho.

Greetings — Salud!

CHARLES, etc.

139

From Spanish Trenches

April, 1937

Salud!

A great deal has happened since I last wrote to you.

I am writing this in a country villa that was formerly owned by the royal family — a choice collection of drooling idiots.

I got a couple of explosive bullets in my left arm, just below the shoulder about ten days ago. Paul and Eddie were both with me at the time. Damn them . . . they went over the top, too, and they weren't supposed to do so. Both of them officers in charge of the assaulting Infantry company. If they had both been knocked off it would have been a serious loss. But neither one was injured. By God! They're brave guys. The way they have fought all through it Paul with a grim, relentless courage, that knows no retreat. Ed with a dashing, almost reckless bravery. Frank I have not seen in action. But they tell me that before he was wounded (he's still convalescing) he was the most sound and responsible leader in the battalion. He also knew no fear.

Gosh, Betsey, you'd be proud of your gang.

Frank, you know, was wounded some time ago. One in the arm and a couple in the leg. He's convalescing at some sea-side resort. Paul was wounded, too, you know, but it was just a flesh wound, and he was back in the line in no time. You'd hardly recognize him now. He's as slim as a chorus girl and a flash of lightning for speed, especially when food is being served. He calls himself variously "the thin man," "Thundercap Burns" etc.

Just received a letter from Frank. Paul and Ed got it first at the front and they relayed it to me. It makes everybody laugh. A good letter.

Ever thine,

CHARLEY

Albacete, Spain

Dear Girls:

I am writing this the same night as my other letter. I am awfully sorry you didn't receive any of my letters and perhaps worried about me. I am well, also Charlie is fine. Paul is here wise-cracking.

I am sorry to say Francis is not here with us. But he was wounded slightly last month. He had a couple of flesh wounds in the leg, but

I now hear from fellows that saw him in the hospital that he is walking around with not a sign of a limp and keeping the hospital in an uproar with his humor. He should be with us in a couple of weeks.

Paul was wounded slightly in the right arm. He recovered very quickly and is now back on the front with us.

I suppose by this time you have received my other letters. In case you haven't I will go over some of the things I wrote before.

I joined Charlie, Paul and Francis the last part of January. We were attached to the Irish section (James Connolly Unit) of the Lincoln Battalion. This Army certainly appreciated the worthiness of the Flahertys for we rose steadily. We all started as plain rank and filers.

Francis was the first to be promoted. That was as Political Commissar of a company. Then Francis was appointed Assistant Company Commander.

Charlie was a bit slow in rising as he was sick with a cold for about a week. Then I was made group leader, then Assoc. Section commander, and now I am a company commander. Charlie is now Political commissar of my company and Paul is Political commissar of the Irish Section. How we doing?

We haven't seen Francis since he was wounded but won't he be surprised at these developments.

We are on a very important front here. But it is now very quiet. The fascists are on their last legs. The American Battalion is a great outfit. It is an International Brigade all its own.

One of the Irish lads received a package from home today and gave us some English cigarettes and chocolates. Charlie is walking around as though full of opium. He puts a piece of chocolate in his mouth and then goes off into flowering phrases of delight. It is wonderful chocolate. Do you suppose you could manage just one bar of Nestle chocolate or even a penny bar? Charlie's day is complete if he can nibble on a piece of chocolate or a tiny hunk of candy.

In regard to American cigarettes, they would certainly be welcome. But stress the candy angle. We are slowly developing a taste, no, not a taste, but a learning to tolerate the Spanish cigarettes. They are awfully strong and hard to keep lit.

The weather has been bad here for a few weeks. Rain and cold.

From Spanish Trenches

The olive trees are very plentiful here, but you can't eat them
They are black olives and the hillsides are lined with them in ter
raced rows. The Spanish comrades tell us we will soon have warm
weather. I hope so.

It is hard for me to describe the country. We are on a hill that
looks back into a beautiful valley. The hills around here do not look
like the hills in Maine. Spain is an old country and therefore there
are no forests. One doesn't see those small rippling streams or roar-
ing mountain brooks of Maine. All land is under cultivation. Even
the mountain tops. Or should I say hill tops — for you couldn't
call these hills mountains.

When the sun shines one can see for miles. And it makes one realize why the Spanish workers and peasants are putting up such a
heroic battle and why they are so determined to drive fascism out of
such a lovely country.

We don't get any snow here but it certainly can get cold about
4 o'clock in the morning. We have plenty of blankets and have a
fine dugout. The food is excellent and no one goes hungry. The
Spanish people sacrifice a lot to see that the men at the front are
well clothed and fed. So continue your good work in raising food and
clothing for Spain.

In regard to the language. Charlie is not the Spanish speaker he
considered himself. He has been grossly misrepresenting himself all
these years. Once in a while he remembers some word or phrase and
loudly repeats it at every opportunity. But when it comes to a question of, say, asking for a cigarette, he, like the rest of us, has to fall
back on the old Indian sign language.

Well, I think I have written enough for one night. So I think I
will close. Again I repeat, it was a joy to receive those three letters
from you. Send some more photos of yourself and DON'T WORRY.

The fascists are on the run so it won't be long before we will be
talking your ears off with accounts of our great doings. So Love to
you all.

Ed

Room 171, Soccorro Roja, Albacete, Spain

Dear girls,

Got your letter dated March 10th yesterday. That's the one you

142

started "Thoughts while not strolling." A good letter, indeed. Send us some more of those. It's a big occasion when we get a letter. Paul and I devoured it. Ed had seen it just before we got it while on the way to the hospital. Now, now, don't get excited. He just had a touch of the grippe. He'll be back in a few days. Now Paul has taken over his job as commander of the company. I'm the political leader of the company.

Frank you know was a company commander before he was wounded. Please *don't* get the *idea* that he's badly hurt. The last time I heard about him he was skipping about the hospital keeping the doctors, nurses, etc., in continual laughter. Paul also received a slight flesh wound in the arm about a month ago. He's been back here now for three weeks or so. Ed and myself — nary a scratch. And *no* possibility of getting one. This sector we're in now is as quiet as Sunday afternoon in Machiasport, Maine.

The fascists are deserting to our lines every day. Our airplanes and tanks are wonderful. The job they do on the enemy is stupendous — in fact, it's a caution!

Judging from the great victories we are achieving on the Guadalajara and other fronts, it won't be long before we completely rout them. And how they'll run when once they start! There's very little enthusiasm for fighting among the fascists opposite us. A short while ago one of our Spanish comrades stood up in the trench with his head and body up to his waist above the parapet, and shouted to the enemy troops, urging them to shoot their officers and come over to us. He talked to them and he beckoned them for fifteen minutes. They saw him. They could have easily shot him, but not a bullet was fired. That night twenty-five of them came over.

We've received about three *letters* from you altogether. Again I caution you not to expect letters regularly from us and not to worry if you don't hear from us for long periods. I suppose Frank has been writing to you from the hospital or where he's convalescing.

It isn't too warm here yet, by any means, but I expect to be comfortable soon.

Eileen and Mary must be growing fast. Our love to them.

Ernest Hemingway and J. B. S. Haldane were here a couple of days ago. Both of them are real men.

Last Monday evening we held an Easter Week-James Connolly

commemoration meeting right here on the front lines. A committee composed of members of the English and American Battalions arranged the meeting. It was a gala event. Ed was the song leader and we had Irish songs galore. We have plenty of musical talent around here. More than we could use in one night. Our Battalion commander is an Irish-American. Knows his Irish history, too. He was one of the speakers at the meeting. I told you before, didn't I, that we had quite a few I.R.A. men with us? They're the best soldiers.

Paul says, "Remind Dorothy that her birthday and mine are on the same day. Would that we could observe it together. Save a piece of cake for me. Don't lap the frosting off! Salud! No Pasaran! and Erin Ga Bragh (Will you join me in a bowl of John Jameson?)"

Food coming now and Paul & I have tremendous appetites. This letter must close.

Love to yez all,

CHARLEY

One of the close relatives of David and Sheldon Jones writes:

"The love of liberty that prompted the ancestors of David to embark on the Mayflower in search of a land of freedom in the early part of the 17th century, moved David and Sheldon Jones, in 1937, to join the Abraham Lincoln Battalion to fight for Spanish democracy." David is 39, Sheldon a few years younger. Their parents owned a prosperous New England shoe factory. Later they lost their fortune. Both David and Sheldon enlisted in the Navy during the World War, both served on the "Florida."

Somewhere in Spain, Feb. 22, 1937

I have experienced my first air-raid. The town where I am working was heavily bombed in an attempt to destroy our factory. The women and children suffered the worst losses. It seems as though they tried on purpose to bomb the closely populated district. It is frankly terrifying when the bombs come down out of the air with a whistling noise that is even stronger than the whirr of the engine. I think the most disturbing element about raids is that one has nothng to do but wait and see where the bombs land. And it was our good luck that they missed us. I think though it was hardest upon the women and children.

The food is fine and the people are very friendly to us and considerate in every way. Their morale seems' very good despite all attempts to terrorize them which fail. Their courage is remarkable.

SHELDON JONES

(Sheldon Jones to his son, 9 years old)

Somewhere in Spain, Feb. 24, 1937

Dear Son:

I am here working on my job. It is a fine one; the best I ever had. Your uncle has already gone on his. I am working with many French, German and Spanish workers and I find it quite difficult not being able to speak and read these languages and now I have to study very hard to learn them. Remember, son, learn as many languages as you can. French is a good one to start with.

I saw a whole train load of refugees from Málaga and had time to talk with some of them. They were mostly women and children and old people. They told me that as they were getting on the train at Málaga, a Fascist plane came down very low and opened fire on them with machine guns. Several were wounded.

All the people that I've talked with are very bitter towards the traitor General Franco — he has no sympathy from any Spaniard that I've met. And as for the Germans and Italians they regard them quite naturally as foreign invaders which in truth they are. The general attitude here among the people is strongly anti-fascist, so strong in fact that all old differences among the people are disappearing in their one great determination to crush completely the fascist invaders and traitors.

By the time that Fascism is beaten here, all the world will despise these Fascist brigands.

Good-night, son, and know that I am proud of such a son and comrade.

FATHER

From Spanish Trenches

Dear Edith:

As you no doubt remember in the days of my very callow youth I helped to make the world "Safe for Democracy" only to find out afterwards that I and 20 million others, more or less, were just plain goats. Two years in Arizona convinced me entirely and completely how dreadfully we'd been "stung."

I came here because I thought that as an American it was my duty to support, to the best of my ability, a people struggling for their elementary rights and freedom from age-old oppression.

I have seen enough to convince me that their cause is just and then some. I have seen the terrible havoc of the bombing of civil populations. The price is paid by women and children — women crushed to death clutching their babies in their arms — wanton destruction, machine gunning from the air of helpless refugees (again women, children and aged.)

Don't for a moment let yourself be deluded into believing that the present situation in Spain was brought about by a lot of radicals; that is a fabrication out of whole cloth. The great mass of the people are wholeheartedly back of their government. The tales of vast hordes of Russians are false. There are some technicians, but no substantial number. The amount of volunteers as compared to the number of Spanish loyal troops appears to be insignificant, though they've had a great moral value.

Madrid will be the downfall of the German and Italian fascists if they persist in their aggression.

I cannot see any basis for anyone failing to support the Spanish people who has the slightest regard for Democracy and all that it implies of possibility for education, progress and development, all of which was stifled under the old regime. It seems to me also that a curb must be put up against Nazi aggression and Mussolini's black shirts unless the world is to be thrown back into the dark ages. When I see you I'll be able to tell you far more than I've space or time to write.

If you think it wise give my love to Auntie Belle and all the family.

SHELDON

The U.S.A.

April 21, 1937

Dear Bess,

A comrade is writing this letter for me, as my right wing is temporarily on the shelf. However, it is nothing serious, and I expect the next missive will be in my own illegible hen-scratch.

Just now I have been given a soft job. This usually happens to a pick and shovel expert when his best wing is on the hog. There is a great premium here on letters and one from you is priceless.

Now, Bess, to get down to brass tacks. You made a reference to the possibility of your coming over here. I think you should come over as soon as you can, and advise bringing the papoose too. This is going to be the world's second greatest country — the present phase cannot last long, and there is not too much time to become acclimated and to learn the language, in order to be of maximum usefulness. You will be able to find out the proper channels easier than I can.

So far I have not been able to see Sheldon, but have heard of him directly through a number of people, who know that he is well and happy.

The spirit of our boys is very big, and things are changing for the better every day in almost every field of activity.

Well, dear, think over carefully what I have suggested, and I hope you see fit to act soon and favorably.

Remember me to all our friends. I can't tell you how tickled I am with the progress your mother has been making. Take that as a barometer — if she can come 'round toward our way of thinking, then many others are also changing. No doubt if you can come over in the near future, we can have much time together,

Love,

(am signing with left hand)   DAVID

ROBERT MUNSON TAYLOR is a Boston lad of 22. He lost his mother when he was three and was brought up by his grandmother, who belonged to the D.A.R. and the Colonial Dames. Her brothers fought in the Civil War. Grace is his sister.

From Spanish Trenches

Hello Tank:

How are things going with you and Gramp. I feel a bit louzy over the way I had to tell you I was going to S.A. I suppose you know by now that I am in Spain fighting the Fascists.

You will think no doubt that I am a damn fool for coming, but someday you will realize how right I was. If you yourself could come over here and see the situation there would not be one iota of doubt as to whether or not I was right. This war is twice as horrible as the last. It is incredible to think that modern science could have invented such new and deadly weapons for the destruction of man by man.

The Fascists are beasts in the employment of these and at the front it is not an uncommon sight to see men burning from incendiary bullets.

The machine guns fire exploding bullets that will blow a man's head from his shoulders. The Fascist's bombers come over and bomb towns filled with women and children and at one town the kids had scars on their faces from bomb shrapnel. The planes in this war can go 400 miles an hour while the bombers can do 275 m.p.h.

Once in the trenches we were bombed twice. There, fascist's bombers supported by about 30 pursuit planes came over and I could see the bombs leave the bottom of the plane and drop down. The nearest one landed about 50 feet from the trenches which shows how louzy they are. One day we were shelled for five hours steadily, but after the 2nd hour we started a card game and every time we heard a close one coming we thumbed our nose.

So far we have been beating the fascists to hell, but they are in a funny position. Most of them are Germans or Italians and if they want to quit they find an officer ready to shoot them. Every day we had anywhere from 30 to 60 deserters coming over to our side and they would tell stories of torture that would have chilled the heart of Bluebeard. After a day's fighting we could not leave any wounded on the field because at night the Moors and Germans would come out and knife them. Several times we found lads who had only slight wounds with their necks slit open.

There is one thing however that our lads have got that the Fascists haven't and that is Courage. You should see some of the Spanish kids of 16 or 17 years run out, climb up on top of a tank and heave a hand grenade into the peep hole. Most of the Spanish men are at the front and they are a swell bunch. The women treat us swell and they do a million and one things for us such as washing, sewing, etc.

This country is beautiful too and the climate is swell. During the early afternoon it gets so warm that all the shops close and everyone takes a Siesta, even the animals. The wine here is excellent and I'm quite accustomed to getting along without water.

I am writing this from a hospital. I was slightly wounded on the 27th Feb. when I went over the top. I feel pretty good now and expect to return to the front any day. When I do I'll give those Fascists a good dose of American Hell. Well, Tank, you and Gramp take things easy and the next time I go out I'll pick a couple of oranges for you.

Lots of love,

Bob

March 6, 1937

Dear Grace:

I don't know if they told you I was killed in action or not but last Saturday (Feb. 27) our Battalion went over the top and after things had cleared up I was reported dead. The truth of the matter is that I received a brain concussion and laid for three days in a hospital not knowing where I was. When I came to I found that three English chaps had found me wandering around in a daze and had taken care of me. They were wounded also and it was damned nice of them to see to me.

I don't know what happened to me but from the bumps on my head and the way it hurts I think that a shell must have landed quite near me. I feel a lot better now and expect to return to the front any day. Paul was here but left for the front last night. He was only slightly wounded.

I am a section leader and in the two times that we went over the top my section has almost been wiped out. The first time out of 42 men I had 23 left and the second was when I got mine but I was told that there were only 10 or 11 left from 42.

From Spanish Trenches

That day we went over I saw three of my boys get it. One was cut in two by machine gun fire another got three right through the head and the third was dead before he hit the ground. One of the lads was lying by my side when he got it and as long as I live I shall never forget that sight. I have been at this hospital for the past two days. The Dr. just told me that I leave for the front tonight.

If I go I'll give those fascist bastards a dose of their own stuff.

Give my regards to all the gang and tell Mike that there is plenty of work over here for guys like him.

So-long,

BOB

April 20, 1937

Dear Phil:

A thousand apologies for not writing to you before this but did not think it advisable. You know Phil the lads from Boston are swell and hold some of the best positions. Ed Flaherty is Company Commander and his men would go through hell and high water for him. Paul Burns is Assistant Co. Commander and he too is admired by the men. Sunky and Chas. Flaherty have been wounded and are both in the hospital. You know with those two fighting romantic Irishmen it's a question which has the most attraction for them: the beautiful nurses or the front line with its bullets and shells.

Phil doesn't it make your heart burn when you see how England and the U.S. are stabbing Spain in the back with their non-Intervention and Neutrality Acts? If only the working class of these countries could see the situation in its right light. If they would only ignore the reactionary reports of Hearst and the other capitalist papers and read the true story of Spain. If they would only see the true light what an easy job we Anti-Fascists would have, but as they don't we must work like hell until a *true* democracy is established throughout the world.

At present we have the enemy on the run on all fronts and the situation looks very good. The next move in the International situation is up to Mussolini and no matter which way he moves England has the opportunity to check-mate him. But will she?

I wish you could see some of these Fascist deserters that come over

150

o our lines every night. They are mostly Italian lads who have been lured to Spain so that Mussolini may feather his nest with the blood of Spanish peasants. The very lackadaisical way they fight proves to us that their stories of being forced to fight are true.

We on the other hand are Idealists fighting for something which we know to be right in every degree.

The deeds of heroism which we perform in the name of Anti-Fascists amaze those soldiers who were in the last war. Every bullet we fire and every grenade we throw is done so with a fervent hope that we will avenge some of those civilians slain by Fascist bombs. I think Sherman said "War is Hell," but he never had to stand up against the International Brigade or else he'd have put it much stronger than that. Every nation in the world is represented in the International Brigade.

Well, Phil, the candle grows dim so I'll have to close. Give my best greetings to all the gang.

Salud!

Bob

BEN LEIDER, 35 years old, was probably the first American killed in Spain.

He left a well paying job as newspaper correspondent to fly for the Spanish Government. This was at a time when the Government had only the poorest, most inadequate, and most antiquated planes. He writes to his brother.

Murcia, January 31, 1937

Dear Will:

I have just come back from a few drinks with some *companeros* from back home and I am in the mood for taking a firm stand like a moth-eaten statesman and making resounding statements.

As bad as I've turned out from the point of view of "practical" considerations, my safety margin is still greater than yours. For reasons which you may guess I can't be more specific about myself, but things are happening fast; in fact, in a few days they will develop all of a sudden for me. In my own way, I am meeting my own requirements for peace of mind and self-respect.

From Spanish Trenches

Sometimes I am as much in the dark here about the progress of the fight as you are at home. But I have seen tangible developments here in the direction of discipline, fighting spirit, skill, etc. which is beginning to set the Spanish people apart from other down-trodden peoples. And wherever I go — and I go places — I see evidences of deeprooted social changes taking place which cannot be accounted for merely by some educational or propaganda program. This isn't Germany's Abyssinia. Something is going on here which the people have wanted for decades — and they are recognizing it as it happens! Once they get the idea, you can't kill it with bullets. The presence of the International Brigade — a growing force drawing its strength from those who are Frenchmen, Germans, Italians, English, Austrians, Czechoslovaks, Americans, etc. — speaks for the new line-up. Even after you make the necessary realistic deductions, you can say of that force, here is something which has happened for the first time in history.

An interesting sidelight on the activities of the Brigade is the universal disgust with the silly language difficulties the various units have. It's just another lesson in fundamentals.

There are no children running wild here as the result of the strife. The kids here often remind me of Irene, Billy and Jimmy — which is a cheerful and hopeful thought to close with.

My love to all.

BEN

P.S. Tell the folks you heard from me.

ED ERIK is a young New Yorker who was active in the League against War and Fascism before leaving for Spain early in 1937.

April 26, 1937

Dear Louise:

Another stab at the Battalion typewriter. I had a lot that I wanted to say in my last letter that I didn't because I was in such a hurry. How I could have missed telling you of Spring in this country, tho, is still beyond me. Another trip from the front lines for a while (to take a shower) reminded me that I should.

The U.S.A.

The difference between the front, where the trees have been ruined by shell and rifle fire or been used for construction or heating purposes, and slightly to the rear is amazing. About one or two miles to the rear of us is Morata de Tajuna. When we arrived at this front the town was deserted and filthy. It had been taken from the fascists only a few days previous to our arrival. Now that it seems certain that the fascists "shall not pass" the town is slowly being repopulated. The garbage is being cleaned away and normal life, commercial life excluded, is being resumed. Trees of all sorts are in bloom. I don't know the names of them but they certainly are pretty. There's lavender, pink and various colored blossoms to add to the constant green of the olive trees. Poppies are also in bloom. I wish I was a bit more capable of describing these things. Reading of them can never have the same effect as seeing it.

As for myself, I'm still here. My sergeant was hurt in a truck accident and I'm temporarily filling in for him. Meaning that I'm probably next in line for the sergeancy. I've got a coat of tan, a mustache (which I'm shaving off on my next shave), and clean underwear (I took another shower today). The boys chipped in and bought a radio and three loudspeakers, which does help relieve the tension of being at the front for the length of time we've been here. Reading material has been brought up, and, believe it or not, most of it is the English version of America's famed Street and Smith publications. We get news bulletins every day here. I've just read about those nurses who went on strike receiving five to twelve years. Add my protests — and make them plenty sharp.

Please write and ask the others to. It means a lot here, even to an old knocker-abouter as myself. And so

Salud,

ED

HANK is most easily described as a New Yorker. A life in the city, poring over books and papers, left him rather baldish and flat-chested at the age of thirty-eight. He earned an excellent livelihood as a publicity man. His letters are to his wife, to the wife of his best pal and to other friends who worked with him in the American Writers' Union in New York.

153

From Spanish Trenches

Murcia, Spain, March 28, 1937

Dear Helen:

I was suddenly pulled out of the station near the front and attached to a hospital here which is quite a distance away. In the switch I was detached from Ralph and I have no idea where he is. News travels slowly in Spain and it probably will be months before I meet him again. As things go . . . and as long as I am attached to this detail I am in practically no danger. I pull a truck around, go to the abattoir, to the market, haul convalescent comrades around and occasionally bring in wounded. And as the saying goes "To him who hath shall be given." Here I am living a softer life than even America had to offer and I get three damn good meals a day, sleep in a real bed with real sheets and am stuck into a town which just oozes beautiful senoritas at every squeeze. So far it's a grand war.

However it has its other qualities too. Naturally it is boring and I think that as soon as I can fix it I will try for a transfer to the front. Seeing wounded comrades coming in makes you feel a bit aaah about this sort of existence.

But through it all I see Spain and I know now, although I only surmised it from reading between the lines in the bourgeois press that Franco can only ravage Spain. How he can hold the people down on his rear guard is indeed surprising and how long he can do it without Hitler and Mussolini does not need much deduction. The people in a body are for their democracy. And to see a people in this transitory stage is something that you can never forget, once you are part of it.

On all the stores, on the buses, at the slaughter house, in the marketplace are signs reading "Controlled by the workers." They have certainly knocked capitalism into a cocked hat in short order here.

And when I see some of our American comrades who have been wounded and hear stories about white collar workers side by side with manual workers going over the top without a murmur (the most struggle any of them have had has been an occasional pinch on a picket line, although they faced danger as extreme as any world war soldier ever saw) I begin to change my opinion of the uselessness of the intellectual. There are stories of heroism that are truly epic . . . and they will be read and retold sometime.

154

My Spanish is progressing at a standstill pace. Between trying to make myself understood in a patois of German, French and English (Why the hell don't we internationalists go in for Esperanto?) and taking orders in French my little brain is in very much of a whirl. However I suppose I will get there. Incidentally no Applejack yet. I'm living on cognac which you can get here at about one cent a shot and I get the equivalent of thirty cents a day with tobacco thrown in so even Ira could get along in this man's army.

If the Union wants to do something let them get about fifty bucks' worth of American cigarettes (you can get them for about five cents a pack if they are for export — no tax). Send them to the American Battalion of the International Brigade, Albacete. The guys are simply walking about with their tongues down to their boots. If you ever smoked a French cigarette or tried to smoke a Spanish butt you'll know what this will mean to them.

Did I say before that I think Spain is one hell of a good place to live in? I'm considering remaining here. Wanna come?

My love to you and to everyone else I know. "Salud!"

Love,

HANK

Murcia, Spain, April 2, 1937

Dear Helen:

Sometime when we are together, reading the Encyclopedia Brittannica on the cold winter evenings that you nincompoops put up with in the States (Gosh ain't I getting European?) I'll tell you what chicanery and charlatanery and buggery I have to go through to get the use of this typewriter which is the inventor's working model, without a doubt. But it *is* a typewriter and it makes letter writing almost a pleasure.

Life here in this lovely land goes on for me and it gets more and more interesting. I have been on two swell assignments . . . one to a little fishing village on the Mediterranean in order to buy fish for the hospital, and eggs and meat from the country side. Part of the trip took us to within twenty miles of the fascist lines but I didn't know, from the appearance of the people and the calm and peacefulness that I was so near to grim war until I returned and saw a map.

I saw a bit of Spain that I never would have seen if I had journeyed here on my own hard earned dollars. We went up a mountain side on roads that wound around in such a way that it seemed as if the headlights would bump into the tailboard. On one side was a continuous precipice with a drop of at least one thousand feet . . . and towards the top of the mountain much higher. It was very thrilling. After the mountains we came upon a very fertile plateau dotted here and there with farms whose buildings showed that they were many hundreds of years old. We talked to the farmers and then as if by telegraph farmers came from all over to sell us eggs and chickens. They surely know how to manipulate the grapevine telegraph in Spain. On the way we came across a school with the children out in the yard for recess. I stopped to take their pictures and they all started singing the International, greeting me with the upright clenched fists. I probably have told you about the kids here in previous letters but pardon the repetition. I'll probably be thrilled enough by the sight to keep telling you about it as long as I write to you. You better settle down to it now. You will undoubtedly have to put up with a hard hot summer and a long cold winter of it.

There is an interesting story that some of the wounded tell about a bunch of Moors who came to attack our lines singing the "Internationale" . . . the boys thought they were comrades until almost the last moment when they discovered what was really up and gave it to them. I don't know whether you have heard much in America about what the Abraham Lincoln Battalion has been doing, but here they give it credit for having stood up against probably the most vicious attack of the war and after the attack (and very many of our boys are not here now) they had actually advanced their fortified positions. Some of them were rushed into the front with practically no training but they did learn quickly.

At the little fishing village (to get back to my original story) there were a group of girls, socialists, republicans, and communists who are working day and night sewing uniforms, shirts and bandages for the wounded. We were really the folks of the hour (I had gone out with two other comrades, one a Belgian and the other a

156

British boy who had been wounded quite severely but is now practically well). They came from all over town to greet us, buy us drinks and to try to tell us how grateful they were for the International Brigade. We spent two days on the outing.

And then the old Hank's luck holding out, I rated another trip, this time with a German.

This letter is being written in sections. Yesterday just as I got to the end of page 1, I was called out to take a group of boys to a convalescent home about a hundred kilometers away (a kilometer to you, my dear, is five-eighths of a mile). I stayed there last night and returned this morning. A very nice little jaunt and went simply cuckoo over a young Spanish girl at the place I took the comrades to. However this means nothing because you see I no spikka da Espanol and she can only tell by the hungry look in my eye that I am putting the bee on her and that, as the Germans around here say, "*gibte garnichts.*"

Yesterday I left off telling you about a trip I took with a German. This guy was a member of the Reichstag and was pinched along with Thaelmann and spent thirty months in a concentration camp. He managed to escape finally, spent some time in Holland and then came here. Incidentally the 20th of April is Thaelmann's birthday and there is a battalion of the International Brigade named after him, composed of Germans, many of whom escaped from concentration camps and others who came out of Germany directly. If you can imagine what this means you will understand why I think that we should do something especially for them. It is impossible for them to get mail from home, or little contributions such as cigarettes, etc. It might be a swell idea to get people in America to keep up correspondence with individual members. It would be swell for morale. See whether you can do it.

I am getting very much in demand here for my typewriting ability. I translate the news from French into English for the bulletin and because of this I have the privilege of using the machine when it is free. I am now starting a novel, really and honest to God in earnest and I think it will be something.

How are all the boys and girls? And you? And have you a job? I'm being pulled away again so   So long,

                                         HANK

From Spanish Trenches

Dear Bee and Helen:

When Hank says he promptly got a leave of absence and came to the town where I am staying at — when he heard I was there — he puts it mildly. The morning of the day he arrived here our outfit marched fourteen kilometers to indulge in some maneuvers to defend the town in the event of a fascist attack. Well, we theoretically defeated the fascists, but we couldn't hold out against Hank, — he absolutely took the town by storm.

Regards to all of you,

PETE

Dear Helen and Bee:

I heard of Pete's arrival and promptly wangled two days liberty so that I could see him. He looks swell. We've been swapping stories for about two hours and now I'm leaving for my post, which is about seventy-five–eighty miles away from here.

How are the chances of our seeing you here? Can't you get over with the Writer's ambulance?

Love to you both,

HANK

International Hospital, Apasionaria, Murcia, Spain
(——, 1937)

Dear Harry:

My fighting in this war was as vastly different as I expected it would be . . . and Spain too, for that matter, is totally different than anything you could imagine by reading accounts of what goes on here in the New York Times. The news has probably come to you that at last I'm completely out of the intellectual sphere and that I am now a true proletarian driving a truck. To hear me swear at gypsy caravans and Spaniards burdening the hind quarters of little donkeys while they blithely block the road you would think that I had been earning (!) my living at this for years and years.

Although I have been quite near the front on several occasions I have yet to hear my first bombardment and from the looks of things I doubt whether I will get up near the front for some time to

158

come. In the meantime I am doing useful work (they hold American drivers at a premium here) seeing Spain and working like a s.o.b. The stomach has practically disappeared and biceps are fast forming. When you juggle 200 lb. cases it does get you into condition.

There is little you could want for in a physical way . . . we get swell meals and grand sleeping quarters here (for more than three weeks before I came to Murcia I slept on good hard boards with an excuse for a mattress thrown on them) with real beds and white sheets. The pay is good, six pesetas a day which in American means approximately fifty cents. But whereas at Harry's fifty cents will only drag two applejacks, here you have to know higher mathematics to figure how many cognacs would be thrown across the bar. Cigarettes are issued but if you have to buy them they cost a little more than half a peseta.

I recall the conversations we used to hold about Spain . . . and wondered why Franco could have pushed as far as he did. When you get here the answer is simple. If it weren't for Hitler and Mussolini his forces would collapse like a house of cards. At the beginning the Spanish workers were simply overwhelmed by superior forces and the newest weapons of war. It took time to train troops and to get war materials. You can see now what the Spanish people are doing, once they caught their breath. Here back of the lines you see a spirit that is simply amazing. People who have lost brothers, sons and fathers go about their work actually smiling. Nothing seems to stand in between them and their daily tasks. There is a feeling of class consciousness I think you would find in no other country . . . and I am not excluding Russia. For Russia is almost a generation removed from her basic struggle against imperialism. You see signs on shops, on railway trains, on the buses "Controlled by CNT" which is the equivalent of AF of L . . . CIO. They sing at their work . . . and this phantasy of manana seems to have gone out with the coming into power of the Front Populaire. I've seen Spanish craftsmen turning out work that an American artisan would be proud to produce. Franco must be having a hell of a time keeping the South of Spain under control!

Sometime I'll tell you the story of how I got into Spain . . . it's a thriller if ever there was one. But at any rate I can tell you now that it felt like the millennium when I heard a bunch of school-kids singing the "Internationale" in Catalonian on this side of the border . . . and to see little tots of two and three raise their clenched fists in salute.

The countryside is beautiful. Spain is very mountainous, at least this part — all around are orange and lemon trees in bloom. Days are warm but not too warm. Nights are cool. It will be a grand place to live when we finish what the fascists started. And at the present time I am almost convinced that I shall remain here.

So far I've given you the brighter side of the picture. I see plenty of the other as well. I am attached to a hospital and I see many boys I knew home here, wounded. Some have died. This business here isn't just heroics. It is pretty sordid in spots. Seeing comrades who have just come out of the line gives you a picture of the war that you in America can't quite grasp. Those who have served in the World War say that it is much more terrible. And you must know that whenever you hear about battles that the figures given in casualty lists are not just numbers . . . that a great number are your own comrades in the International Brigade. You must do much more for Spain in America.

I feel like I'm on a soap box but I was particularly touched today. The brother of an English comrade, recuperating at the hospital, died and I took a bunch of the wounded to the funeral.

So much for this war. What I am dying to hear is news from home. Please write me, and do it often. And don't for goodness' sake wait for mail from me. This week I've had some spare time in the evenings. It may be weeks before I get such a break again.

Give my love to Roy and to Bert. I've taken some pictures which are being developed now. I'll send you some when they are finished.

Love.

HANK

International Hospital, Murcia, Spain, April 14, 1937

Dear Bee:

Your boy friend is a sergeant and although in this man's army sergeants don't hurl expletives in the manner in which an American non-com does, still to be a sergeant means that the men want him and respect him. So much for that. Little Pete pushes his boys around, with the faintest vestige of a mustache on his upper lip, brown as a berry and fit as only the simple life (bed at ten and reveille at six) could make him. He looks swell.

For me life is grand. I'm living better than I ever did in America . . . I heartily recommend Spain to all those intellectuals who need a change and rest for their jaded nerves. And I must admit that the kick so lacking in America is here at an ever increasing pace.

. . . But this I want to stress . . . anything that you or the Union can do for this fight should be pushed with everything you've got. I, for one, don't see why the boys and girls of the firm can't give a day's pay for the ambulance. If you'd see some of the wounded that were piled into insufficient space and came through actually with grins! A Polish doctor was bragging about one of his American patients who told him everything was OK, although he had a hole in his back big enough for you to stick your fist into, and a temperature of 104. Today he's walking around. So you see if we have the ambulances we can save a lot of the boys . . . I think also that if you do get together on an ambulance it might well be named after . . . . . ., who is missing in action (you know what that means). . . . I'm beginning to get a bit soap boxy, but you'll have to excuse it. I'm attached to a hospital, you know, and I see much. The veneer went by the boards a few weeks ago.

I can't tell you how much I miss all of you. I don't get a chance to see many of my American comrades here at the hospital. I speak and actually think in a potpourri of foreign languages. It leaves plenty of time at night to think back of the times we all had together at home . . . and to get sentimental and wonder how many of us will be together to continue them.

I'm coming back to America for a while because I think I may be of some use, but I'm almost convinced that I will make my home here in Spain after it is over. And I've the place all picked out. It's a little town called Aguilas on the Mediterranean with jagged cliffs overlooking the blue, blue sea. Little fishing boats go out every night and come in with their haul in the morning. There are palm trees and orange and lemon groves, and wild poppies grow along the highway. Farmers coddle their goat herds through the old cobbled streets and there ain't a single troubadour around. You buy your victuals in an old market, pile them on your donkey and wind your way up the mountain to where your house overlooks the town. Then you sit up there and WRITE . . . If you want, I'll reserve the next cottage for you.

Immediately, however, I'm pulling a camion around Spain, developing longshoreman's shoulders and arms and quickly (and I hope permanently) losing that fallen chest that adorned me of yore. I'm thinking of taking out a card in the truck drivers union when I get back.

Give my love to every one . . .

HANK

↔

PETE left New York about a month later than Hank, who is his best friend. He left his job to sail for Spain. His letters are to his wife.

March 28, 1937

Dearest Bee:

I've tried to write this letter at least four times in the last four days, but each attempt was cut short by some necessary activity. Today is Sunday and at last I have a chance to get the damn thing off.

We've been moving so frequently and so rapidly we have lost more or less all conception of time. It was only yesterday that I learned the day of the week and the date of the month. There's much to write about. In fact, there's so much I don't know where to begin.

Before I do begin, however, you must understand that in many things I cannot be specific — for military reasons.

Too many well-intentioned people have betrayed the position of an army by carelessly mentioning dates and places.

True, our letters are censored, but if anything is written that even remotely seems informative, from a military point of view, the entire letter is destroyed. The censors cannot take the time to cut a word here and a line there.

The entire trip took about fifteen days, that is, from the time we left to the day of our arrival at the training base.

At times the route was not only difficult but dangerous. Most of suffered minor mishaps, such as bruises and cuts; a few received ore serious injuries, while two comrades were prevented, by mporary injuries, from accompanying us to the very end.

Don't misunderstand. For a bunch of soft city slickers we came rough in fairly good shape. And, by the way, believe me when I rite that the spirit and courage of the group was amazing.

We arrived at the supply base a couple of days ago, and were utfitted with uniforms and the usual army equipment.

Frankly, darling, I'm not a very impressive looking specimen in uniform. Perhaps it's best that you saw me first in my street lothes. However, that's of no particular importance, since I came ere to fight the fascists and not to get myself a wife.

After a fairly good meal (and, incidentally, veterans of previous vars, who are now in the International Brigade, agree that this is he best fed army they ever were in — which is damned important vhen you stop to consider that an army marches and fights on its tomach), we boarded an army truck and started for the training amp, which is in the general direction of the front.

On the way to the camp, the truck in which we were riding suddenly pulled up alongside of the road. A moment later the driver hopped out, ran to the rear and sticking his head into the canvas hastily asked us if we had heard an airplane motor. Since we could barely speak to each other above the rattle of the bumping truck and the roar of its motor, it was to be expected that we would not be able to hear the drone of an airplane motor. So the reply was negative. Our driver then told us to scan the skies carefully so that we might spot the plane, if it was in sight.

All of us responded with alacrity. Some of us jumped out of the truck to look, while the driver rapidly ran up the road a "spit," to where another army truck had stopped. Evidently he wanted to find out whether the other driver had spotted the plane.

Meanwhile, all of us were intently, and, somewhat anxiously, scanning the skies for the possible enemy. Airplanes don't bomb moving trucks very often because moving targets are hard to hit, but, instead, they strafe you with a machine gun, flying low and fast. At such a time the best protection in the open is for the group to scatter and fall flat on their bellies, taking advantage of what natural camouflage they can find.

From Spanish Trenches

Well, the whole goddam thing turned out to be a fiasco. Ther was no bombing, no strafing, because there wasn't any enemy plane Our driver returned and informed us he must have been mistaken However, he was cautious, and he was kind enough to tell us wha to do in case of a raid — after we were all theoretically dead — (The procedure, in case of a raid, which was mentioned above, wa told to us afterwards.)

The remainder of the trip to the training camp was manage with little excitement and much discomfort.

When we got to our destination, which, incidentally, is the train ing camp for the American part of the International Brigade, I im mediately inquired for Hank, J. and L. "Did any of the boys know them? Did they know where they were, so that I could see them?"

Sure they knew them. Anybody and everybody would know Hank, with little description. "And the others? Oh, yes! They all stuck together. Well, where the Hell were they?" I was eager to see them . . . "What's that?" Well, I'll be a . . . . . .! Where do you think they were? All three of them picked out nice soft jobs for themselves, out of all danger, driving trucks from supply bases to the front, back and forth, back and forth. The bastards!

Darling, there's not much more I can write to you about — except that I miss you very much and love you even more. (Note: Censor, if you don't like this paragraph, if you think it's too effeminate, you might try putting some saltpeter in your own food!)

I can't tell you when we'll be moving up to the front, because I don't know. Rest assured that we won't move up until we are ready to give a good account of ourselves. I think I'm going to be assigned to a machine-gun unit. I've already attended my first special class, and already I know how to dismantle and put the thing together.

Well — this is about all — Once more, all my love, all my friendship, all my respect.

PETE

P.S. This letter will take about twenty days to reach you, return mail will also take about twenty days. I may be up at the front or under the ground when your letters arrive at the enclosed address. However, write me a half a dozen long letters, for I'm starving for word from you.

164

The U.S.A.

LEON DAVIS was a friend of mine. He was the most gentle and silent young chap I have ever known. Usually he would sit and listen and just smile. He had come to New York City from a small town, looking for a job. This quiet lad surprised me one day by coming to say goodbye. He told me that he had invested the last of his savings in a ticket to Spain. I think he had only five dollars left over for pocket money when I said goodbye to him on the boat.

April 28, 1937, Albacete, Espana

Dear Leslie:

Today is somewhat of a red letter day for me. And the reason? Well, I have just received my first letter since my arrival in Spain. It is the one written by Bonnie and dated March 21. I am immediately instituting a search for the other letters which seemed to have been misplaced in transit. Need I add how exceedingly pleased I was to receive that one letter.

So much has occurred and such is the pitiable state of my memory that I cannot remember when I wrote last; or at what point I left off the haphazard record of my personal history. For the past month and a half, I had been working rather hard on the Southern Front (Andalusia). (Incidentally, driving an ambulance at the front is much more strenuous and difficult than Hemingway — popularizer of ambulance-driving — would have one believe.) About a week and a half ago, I was slightly wounded by one of those damned bombs, dropped by one of Hitler's Junkerplanes. Nothing serious, however, although it did tend to affect me to some extent mentally. At the present moment, I am at Albacete, doing some rather interesting and, I think and hope, useful work with the Service de Presse.

Concerning the war news, there isn't the slightest doubt but that the Republican forces will win; the time depending to a large extent on the pressure labor and liberal forces both in England and America can bring to bear, demanding the withdrawal of the German and Italian troops, and exposing the infamous Non-Intervention Pact — which sounds swell but which daily permits large shipments of planes and munitions from Hanover to Franco. I know that when one reads of these things in America, the usual reaction

165

is "Well, just so much more propaganda." But when one has seen
German planes, piloted by German aviators bomb a defenseless
city which was not in any sense military, and then machine-gun
the civilians who were fleeing through the streets to the safety of
the fields, the hateful reality of International Fascism is no longer
merely words and the tragic farce of Non-Intervention control of
borders becomes an actual menace. The importance of demanding
an immediate withdrawal of the regular troops both Italian and
German from Spain, and either an effective control to prevent
Germany and Italy from sending planes and munitions or the appli
cation of the most severe sanctions, cannot be stressed too much.

Eh bien, there is no sense in writing what you probably al
ready know. I can assure you, however, that the morale of the
soldiers, who daily make some new advances or succeed in holding
positions to which they have advanced, is of the highest.

And coupled with that is the fact that a large reserve army has
been organized and trained. I wish I could write more, but all mail
is censored, and above all, I do want you to get this letter; so until
I find out just how much of my enthusiasm and observations I can
impart to my letters, I must restrain myself.

Just at this moment a rather unusual thing has occurred. I was
in the Plaza, sipping my vermouth and writing this scrawl, when
suddenly from the radio there came the sound of Mendelssohn's
"Overture to a Midsummer Night's Dream." And I was made
aware once more — as I have been many times — of the overwhelming contrasts, and the imperative need of perspective. In
the preface to his book "Espagne, Espagne!", Jean-Richard Bloch
has pointed out that the present hour is not to the writer or the
historian; not for the meditation over the action but the hour for
action. And the hour is to the correspondent of the war — his book
being a case in point.

I shall have time to write now, and you may expect to hear from
me in the near future. Until then, Leslie, au revoir and with much
love to the children,

Yours,

LEON

The U.S.A.

ABE FELDMAN is one of these dynamic young people who must do something every minute of their lives. He would wriggle in his chair if he were forced to sit down for a minute. Wounded in Spain, his impatience to get better and on the active list again expresses itself in a letter he writes to his friends on the New Masses, where he was helping out before he left New York for Spain.

Dear Everybody:

Fight against fascism *now!* For the cost in lives, pain, suffering is almost, excepting for the durable working class, unbearable.

Hurrah! Hurrah! The American Battalion has advanced more than half a mile against the best-trained murderers that Hitler fascism could ship to Spain. The American boys have shown their guts, ability, willingness to give their all — and some *have* given their all — to fight the terror of degradation and barbarism. So please, for the sake of the working class of the entire world, never stop for one moment in the defense of Spanish Democracy, in the collecting of funds, clearly explaining to the people the meaning of Spain, and follow this with definite actions building the united front against fascism. Please; I cannot stress the importance of the united front as I would like to . . .

I am writing this letter from a hospital bed — a bullet through my right foot, a slight, clean, but very painful wound taking about a month to heal, my eyes half-closed from the anti-tetanus injections, my hands weak from loss of blood — so you will have to excuse the incoherency and the poor script. By the time you get this letter I hope to be back at the front — again doing my darndest to answer not for myself so much as for a young kid lying in the next bed.

Seventeen years old . . . Graduation exercises, parties, hikes, puppy love . . . Gee, life is grand; beautiful! What a myth! What a lie!

This kid has just reached his seventeenth birthday. Emaciated, weak, old — instead of hiking in the hills with his best girl he has been hiking through the mud and filth of the front for the past five months, his "puppy love" a rifle the size of his own body. The only grand and beautiful thing in his life is his knowledge that he, to-

167

gether with the other millions of Spanish anti-fascists, will clear the country of the cannibals of civilization.

Spain cannot be defeated when it can put out such heroes. Those young kids will have their graduation exercises in a free workers' and farmers' Spain.

These murderers are not satisfied with the use of bullets — they use dum-dums — and recently they have perfected a new brain-child of the civilized scientists from Heidelburg University — an exploding bullet!

You have heard of the effects of the dum-dums — a deep, ragged hole. The exploding bullet not only leaves a deep, ragged hole, but smashes to bits all bone structure in the hit part.

The kid was operated upon today from the effects of an exploding bullet. He lost four fingers of his left hand and possibly the use of his entire arm. And yet he lies there — not a whimper — worrying about my foot which has blood on the bandage. He says *"Malo!"* — "Bad!"

Back home there, did I hear someone say he had too much work? He is tired hearing about Spain? Anyway, he has collected a great amount of money ($20) for Spanish democracy and therefore has done his part?

Every one of you must begin to realize the danger of fascism and war — must multiply your efforts 100 percent for Spanish democracy and for the united front in the United States. If they still are not convinced, tell them of the eighteen-year-old young Spaniard who has been fighting since July, wounded three times, lost his brother in action, his father and mother slaughtered at Malaga. Yet while on leave, he is taking part in war manoeuvers to perfect his ability to fight fascism still more courageously and correctly. When he found we were Americans, his face beamed. Here was the great American working class come to support the Spanish people in this strife. He asked me questions about the American Y.C.L., what they are doing, etc., and ended with the statement of fact: "We Spanish youth, American youth, youth of all lands — together — will smash fascism in Spain and then in the rest of the world." Can we fail such courageous, untiring fighters against fascism?

Now a few words about myself. I spent a few very enjoyable hours in Gay Paree and then began the long, tedious railroad travel to our point of destination. The outstanding event was the raising of the right hand by literally hundreds of thousands of French and Spanish people in the Popular Front salute wherever we passed. Think of it — a French traffic cop gave us the salute with the little white club they carry. Upon reaching Spain we went into training and then to the front.

I guess the story of my wound is now in order. We were attacking on a wide front. My group had advanced approximately one hundred and fifty yards, to within one hundred and twenty five yards of the fascist trenches (you can gather from this how close we are — we actually sing and yell slogans at each other during lulls in fighting), when their machine-gun got the range. I heard the bullets bite dust within ten feet, so I took a racing dive for the nearest tree. While in mid-air a bullet hit my foot, knocking me over to my side with the power of a sledge-hammer wielded by a giant blacksmith.

This is funny. While lying wounded, what I thought was a rock hit the right side of my hip and prevented me from sitting for almost two days. When I reached the hospital, I remembered that my glasses were in my right hip pocket. Lo and behold, I noticed two bullet holes in my trousers. Pulling out my eyeglass case, I found a bullet had torn its way through the case, melting the metal frame, smashing the lenses, and casually departing without leaving a scratch on my back.

This fight has taught me more about working-class activity than all I've studied in the past years. I would not have missed this for five such wounds as I have received.

A group of eight from Jugoslavia, the remainder of thirteen who started across the border — I hope the five were killed and not taken alive by the fascists . . . The young twenty-year old boy who is fighting in his second revolution — first as a Socialist in the Austrian Schutzbund, and now as a Y.C.L.er of Austria . . . The many Germans who dared the border guards of Naziland to come to Spain to fight against Hitler and fascism . . . The four Negro boys from Chicago with us — two of whom have already died a hero's death . . .

A Tower of Babel but with one basic difference. Although we speak different languages, we understand our mutual fight and slogan: "Fight against fascism by supporting Spanish democracy."

ABE

169

From Spanish Trenches

JACK KALLEBORN comes from a family of English gentlemen farmers transplanted to the United States. Jack's father became an engineer but Jack himself ran the family farm after several years of agricultural school. Although he had no political opinions, he went to the Soviet Union for two years to study the methods of collective farming. He wanted to know whether this system would work in the United States. He returned to the United States in 1934 and left for Spain toward the end of 1936.

March 20, 1937

Dear Sonia:

Got indirect word of you from Sally's friend at the American base hospital.

Yes, I finally got it. Very interesting being shot. For some strange reason was very much surprised when I was hit.

It was on the 27 of Feb. at 10 a.m. We got the order to go over the top so over we went. We were about forty or fifty yards out when the fascists opened up with a cross fire from machine guns, rifles and rifle grenades. What a fire that was. The machine gun fire was heavier than any experienced in the World War. That's not my opinion but that of officers who went through the World War. To continue I got about fifty yards further, running like hell, when I thought someone kicked me in the leg. Went down surprised and plenty sore. Got up again only to flop once more. The only thing to do was to crawl to nearest shelter and start shooting. By this time enemy fire was so heavy none of us could get any further. There were a lot of killed and wounded on both sides that day.

The worst of it was the fire was so heavy that the first aid men couldn't reach those of us who were farthest out. I had to wait till dark then managed somehow or other to crawl in myself. After the first wound in the leg they hit me three more times. Twice in the right arm (slight wounds) and one graze on the side. That was a lucky one. The fascists are using a lot of explosive bullets. The one that grazed my side struck my cartridge belt right over the gut, exploded and a piece just took off a hunk of skin. But for a freaky stroke of luck would have gone the way of all flesh. Those explosive bullets are barbarous things. I've seen many a head blown wide open by them. They can rip an arm or a leg right off.

170

The U.S.A.

In spite of all this and the fact that on the whole they have superior equipment and better trained troops they haven't been able to make any headway at all. With the exception of Málaga. They have and are suffering loss after loss. Just a few days ago a whole division of Italian troops were practically annihilated and another division sent flying in disorderly retreat at Guadalajara.

They've given us everything they've got and we've stopped them every time. We've seen all kinds of warfare. Been bombed from the air, shelled by artillery, seen aerial dog fights and advanced twice through terrific fire.

We've lost a lot of men but the morale hasn't been affected. This goes for all the loyalist forces and the Spanish people as well. And it's just that which has the fascists licked.

As it looks from here the war will either be over in a short time or else develop into a world conflict. A lot depends on the blockade and the outcome of the present discussions on non-intervention in Spain. Here's where the work for you folks back home comes in. And boy you have lots to do. Now is the time for the workers of all countries to raise more hell than ever before. It's got to be done. Not long ago Albacete was bombed again. One hundred civilians, women and children were killed and three hundred wounded. Spain is doing a heroic job and doing it well in spite of all difficulties, inefficiency and sabotage within our (loyalist, including International Brigade) own ranks, and shortage of supplies. But Spain must be helped, with food and medical supplies and military as well. Though at present we are almost as well equipped as the fascists. Their machine guns are superior to ours. And they happen to be a damned important item in this war.

Remember my qualm over never having had military experience? Well it seems I'm a pretty good soldier. Have been everything from a private to second in command of a company during training period. At the front was in command of a section, forty-two men. The rank might be equivalent to something between a lieutenant and a sergeant.

Wish to Christ I could get out of this bed. Have been on my can for twenty-three days now. Had slight case of lockjaw from anti-tetanus injection which set me back a bit. Funny part of it was I didn't get it till fifteen days after the injection. Boy was that an ex-

171

perience. Couldn't move a muscle and the pain is pretty terrific.
Wound hasn't healed yet but is coming along well. Made a cautious
attempt to walk with crutches but doc says wait a day or two. Expect to be fit for service in three or four more weeks. Seems a hell o'
a while.

My best to all.

JACK

Soccoro Rojo, Room 17.1, Albacete, Spain, April 21, 1937

Dearest Hattie,

What to write about? And you heckle me with demands for details. Other than the general information and the few details I have
already given you, and which you can read in the various presses,
there seem to be no details I can write about.

We are getting the best of care under the circumstances. The doctors and nurses are terribly overworked but the patience and care
with which they treat us is to be marveled at. But fifty-six days in
even the best of hospitals does something to our intellect. Especially when one has been snatched from a fight after being well
started — leaving many scores unsettled. (By the way I'm not the
only one who finds it difficult to write. All the boys complain of the
same thing.) Have been in a convalescent hospital since the thirteenth of this month. It's a beautiful place if one appreciates a date
farm. Thousands of palms, burning sun, millions of flies, very cool,
almost cold nites. And not a blade of grass to be seen. The town is
fairly large. Has a population of 40,000 but there is a provincial air
about it that makes it seem much smaller than it is. It has many
palm shaded squares and sidewalk cafés.

The slow easy-going life of these cafés and squares contrasts
strangely with the rush and roar of trucks and autos dashing about
the streets. The braying of donkeys, sometimes in teams of five
stretched out in single file pulling two-wheeled carts, the shouts of
the muleteers and the cracking of their whips mingles with the
noise of horns and makes a strange music.

The war posters seen everywhere, martial music and militant
speeches coming from a radio in a café or barber shop and the soldiers are the only evidence of war.

The U.S.A.

It's so damned peaceful and I wish I were back at the front. Iave never felt so damned useless. It was a lousy stroke of luck hat took me away on the 29th of February. Shortly after, our attalion saw action that I'd not have missed for anything. Atacks, counter attacks, and when the final tally was taken the fasists had been driven from their strongly fortified position, that we had tried to take, at terrific cost on the 23rd and 27th. There was a dangerous piece of ground between our lines. A few olive trees, then an open stretch. They held a hill that commanded this. It's been rossed and now this front is fairly quiet. They are a bunch of yelow bastards.

April 25, 1937

Don't be angry — I do love you all very much. My slothful naure doesn't allow concentrated mental activity for any length of ime.

Threw away my crutches yesterday. Make my way now slowly and quite surely with a cane. Should be back on the team in a few more days.

Our daily schedule — 8.30 out of bed and wash. 9 a.m. breakfast. 9.30 stroll down town to a café for coffee, sometimes with cognac. Then more coffee until 1 p.m. and lunch. For variation sometimes get myself properly trimmed at billiards. In the afternoon read for a while, we are getting quite a few papers now and a few books. Then downtown for more coffee or billiards until 6.30 when we go to the movies. Nine p.m. supper, 10.30 bed. This wouldn't be bad for a tired guy but a bit tough on a healthy bloke with nothing but a gimpy leg.

Well kid I'm about wound up but remember you asked for details. Jees' you can ask a lot of questions. It's hard to write about details. Up at the front one must try to take things as matter of fact. Those who don't, crack, and it's horrible to see. Others it's pleasanter not to remember. But I'll try to give you a few.

There was one instance, before we left for the front. We were manoeuvering around a trench we had just dug, charging into it from all angles. All the kids were out and having a wonderful time watching us. The only trouble was they wanted to play too and it was a job keeping them out of it. A plane flew over and those kids dug out of there and hid just as fast as they could run. A few sec-

onds later they were back again cheering. "Nuestra, [ours]
fascista." They had seen the red tips on the wings. They ha
learned this lesson well. It is horrible to think of the school in whi
they've been taught. They are the swellest little tykes you've ev
seen. They know just what's going on. One little fellow came up
me and pointing to his jacket and shoes, said "Russo." He jabbere
away evidently trying to find out if I was Russian. When told n
American, he was obviously disappointed but accepted me as th
next best thing.

On the 13th of February we were ordered up. We traveled in
long line of trucks all nite and the next day. Stopped for rifles an
ammunition. Something very reassuring about the feel of a gun an
the weight of a full cartridge belt buckled tight about one's wais
(Out in no man's land, one nite, our belts were almost empty befor
the Amo-echelon [This word unclear] could get through. It's
mighty lonely feeling —)

The trip was long, dusty and tiresome but without incident. E
cept once during the night when the whole convoy stopped and
warning came down the line that any man showing a light would b
shot. Overhead we could hear the drone of heavy bombers. Nothin
happened but we began to feel that we were in the war at last.

When I was ten I floated down a creek full of ice on a log becaus
someone said I didn't dare. Had something of the same feelin
when we neared the front and could hear the artillery and the nois
of a battle and an occasional stray bullet passed.

Our reception at the base was a regal one. We had hardly reache
the place when, as tho staged for our benefit, there was an air raid
Our anti-air craft opened up. High up in the air there were loud re
ports and little clouds of smoke appeared. The fascists climbed fo
healthier air. A few seconds later our planes came over going lik
the hammers of hell. There's nothing more breathtaking than a do
fight. Unless it's a run across country with a flock of machine bullet
on your tail.

We were sent out that night to dig a long line of trench along th
top of a ridge. The fascists were hemmed in on three sides with thei
backs to a river. With no means of communication or of gettin
supplies except over a dangerous bridge. They were in a pretty des
perate position although well fortified and well armed.

174

The U.S.A.

We were tired and sleepy and were really under fire for the first time. It's an awful temptation to hug the ground at first when a hatfull of bullets or a shell goes by. It doesn't take long to get used to it though. As a matter of fact don't know what I'll do back home with no one to shoot at me. By one o'clock that a.m. the sector of trench I was in charge of was finished. The guard was arranged, some of the boys were already asleep. I was smoking a cigarette with my head under a blanket so as not to draw fire. We were feeling comfortable and safe with a nice parapet in front of us. Some one roused me. It was a runner with an order to take my section to another spot and dig some more trench. It can be said, for the morale, that no one grumbled.

We were bombed the next morning. Then shelled. This became almost an every day occurrence. That ridge wasn't exactly a health resort but strangely our losses were small. Most of them from rifle or machine gun fire.

Their planes never did any more than scare the livin' daylights out of us once in a while. They were always in too much of a hurry to get away again. When a heavy bomb explodes near by it almost raises you from the ground and you feel as tho your guts were being sucked clean out. Artillery fire is pretty nasty. But many of their shells are duds. Two struck right in front of the parapet behind which I was lying. Could hear them hiss as they cooled off after striking the ground. Expected to be blown all over the map of Spain. A few minutes later got up to take a look around and was conked in the helmet with a hunk of stone — decided to use my imagination.

About two hundred yards ahead of our trench was an outpost. Some of the boys from my section were stationed there and once or twice a day I would go over to see that everything was O.K. Went over one day about noon. About half way there a sniper put one past my ear and crawling seemed the best way to travel. As soon as I hit the ground a burst of machine gun fire kicked dirt in my face. Didn't wait for any more but scurried like a blinkin' rabbit till I hit the outpost. Had Jesse Owen started with me, on my way back to the main trench, he'd have eaten my dust all the way. The only thing that saved me was that I was a split second faster than the bullets.

From Spanish Trenches

We moved up closer to the fascist's line. Things became more in
teresting. We could see the bastards now and the fire became hotter
But I'll save it for another letter.

War has its humor. One fellow was creased between his stump
and artificial leg. The poor horrified medico almost fainted when the
leg came off in his hand.

Am enclosing photos for you. Your letters are a godsend. Keep it
up, kid. All sorts of love.

JACK

AMERICANS IN SPANISH SKIES

JAMES HAWTHORNE is war correspondent in Spain for The New Masses.

To look at or exchange a few words with such a flier as Frank G. Tinker of Dewitt, Ark. would not lead you to an understanding of the depth of purpose inspiring American participants in this little world war. Tinker looks, talks, and likes to feel pure Arkansas. Tinker (who pronounces his name Tanker) knows there is a Lincoln Battalion in Spain. [Some of the American Fliers in Spain are not attached to the Lincoln Battalion.] Tinker is secretly proud whenever he hears it mentioned by the Spaniards in conversation. But he inquires plaintively, "Why Lincoln Battalion? How about a Jeff Davis Battalion?"

Southern, Annapolis and army-trained, Tinker is no radical. But there is a fundamental fairness to the man that makes him see the justice of organizing sharecroppers to better their conditions even if, as he believed, they too often do not realize that a better life is possible. This same fairness provokes his antipathy to international fascist warfare against the inoffensive Spanish people. Above and beyond mere fairness, and more deeply ingrained too, Tinker has a real American love of independence. That's why he is a fighting democrat; democracy to him spells popular independence and fascism its destruction.

That's what counts with the Spanish airmen, and that's what established Tinker, Jim Allison, Whitney Evans, and Ben Leider of one squadron, and squadron leader Albert Baumler of another, as veritable pets of the air force from the beginning. Professional skill reinforced their position. As human beings they grew close to the native pilots, mechanics, observers, field men, and political commissars.

If the Yank fliers were respected as men and admired as aviators, they won the absolute awe of the ground force as understanding and sincere anti-fascists, defenders of a cause that each understood in his own way but fought for in the same way. Mechanics at Alcalá

177

like to tell about that. One day a disagreement between some Anarchists and Communist mechanics at the field stumped Chimarro, the clever chief of the Communist group. As a rule, the Anarchists, led by a childlike giant, always listened to Chimarro religiously. Tinker's plane needed a new propeller, a job for at least three men. But the angry Anarchists declared that they would not help one another or the Communists. Frank helped his own mechanic for awhile, but the work didn't progress very well. Then he consulted with Jim and Ben and Whitney. They worked out a plan. Together they walked over to the plane, inspected it, discussed it and then broke into a loud and heated argument. Naturally the ground force drew near to find out what was the trouble. The argument got more intense. The Americans, red in the face, walked away in four separate directions. The mechanics asked "Chato," a Spanish pilot on intimate terms with the Americans, what was in the wind. He explained gravely that the Americans had decided not to help one another on the ground or in the air in the future.

The mechanics looked horrified, then sheepish. They didn't need anyone to draw the moral for them. If Spanish mechanics couldn't work together in their own cause, how could they expect foreign volunteers to do so? They went to work on Tinker's plane without a word. At bottom there was the common cause. The rest was chaff.

The Americans had the honor and glory of participating in all the important air work of 1937. On February 4 they did an exhibition flight in which Jim Allison led, Tinker and Evans held the wings, and Leider brought up the rear. They wound up a full bag of tricks with a landing in echelon done perfectly. They found the whole of Albacete cheering when they got down. That was their last exhibition and it was not without military value. But after a few days of bad weather, they went into action on the Madrid front, where their work encouraged the hard-pressed civilian population and the men in the lines.

On February 10, they learned to despise anti-aircraft fire, which burst around their fast biplanes while they protected bombers on two trips against rebel powder factories, and when they descended, on the return trip, to strafe the rebel trenches. The second day of action was more eventful. The rebel ground guns scored a direct hit—the first and only direct hit the Americans have seen since they arrived — against a loyalist plane, which burst into tiny fragments. The "American" squadron (only four were Americans, the rest Spanish) accompanying the bombers on two trips over rebel lines, took revenge. They encircled a fleet of Heinkels and drove them into a nest of government monoplanes which shot down five of the rebel fighters. The rebels were sore, and that night bombed the Alcalá field unsuccessfully. The following day the Yanks again protected the bombers with their biplanes in raids on two railway stations where arms and munitions were accumulated. On the second trip they were boxed by anti-aircraft fire but aside from holes in Tinker's propeller, suffered no damage. Just for luck the monos brought down seven Heinkels.

On February 13, Ben Leider got the first American prize. The biplanes went up at a rocket signal to hunt the fascists over Madrid. The monos got four Heinkels again, and Ben got one. On the fourteenth, great disappointment: the fascists ran! It was not until the sixteenth that the Yanks were able to engage the Italo-German fleet again. The Americans and their eleven biplanes arrived on the Jarama front, where they found twelve Junkers tri-motors, protected by thirty-five Heinkels. With such an advantage, the fascists were willing to fight, but the eleven biplanes paid no attention to the fighters and dived right into the bombers. They brought down two Junkers and, when the Heinkels dived on them, they were joined in a flash by twenty-five monoplanes which got two of the Heinkels before the rest ran away. The squadron was at high pitch, gloating over the rebel defeat on the Jarama, and anxious for trouble. But they couldn't find it. On the Jarama the following day, with nine biplanes, they ran into twenty-four Fiats which turned tail and ran!

On February 18, however, they found trouble — and gave it back. Allison, Evans, Leider, and Tinker in a squadron of eleven ran into a fleet of Heinkels. There were four or five down beneath them for bait and some eighty others high in the clouds — these good divers always fly four or five thousand yards high. Once again the fascists, thinking the squadron was alone were eager to fight. The Americans dived for the low-flying Heinkels and brought them all down. Ben got one and Allison another. As the rebels' huge hid-

179

den fleet zipped down upon them from the clouds, twenty-eight government biplanes spiraled out to reinforce Leider, and the others, while twenty-eight monoplanes ripped into the enemy divers. Allison was wounded twice in the right leg; Ben was hit in both legs. In the meantime seven Heinkels were shot down. Allison landed safely. Leider gritted his teeth and made for the landing field. Tired, taut, he overshot the field and turned to try again. This time he made it, but was so weak he couldn't hold out and came down hard. Luck was against him; the plane was not completely smashed up, but his limp body had crashed against the instrument board. The Americans had given their first life to the cause.

Whitey Evans had to bail out. Cool, calculating he held the ripcord for three thousand feet and he felt he was safe from a cowardly shot in the air. When the parachute opened, it was with a tremendous jerk that gave him a bellyache for a month, but he landed safely and was in the air again the following day! In the air with Tinker to avenge Ben Leider.

BEHIND THE FASCIST LINES

Jamás irán al olvido
Aquellas pascuas pasadas
Inolvidables han sido
Las familiares veladas.

J ust remember, I'll never forget
A ll those Christmas days gone by.
I neradicably stamped in my head
L ovely memories are held high.

The little poem on the photostatic copy of the original Christmas card was not written to inspire sentiment. Its sole purpose was to advise the recipient of the state in which the sender found himself. Read down the first initial of each of the lines, written in red ink in the original to separate them from the rest of the poem.

An American citizen, native of Spain, was forced by failing health to sell his business in the United States. He returned to the sunshine of his motherland to regain his health. In one of Spain's seaports he and his wife lived peacefully as any tourists might. He found a friend in a man who held a position in the Spanish government. How was he to know that this would be considered treason when the rebellion broke out, and the seaport, where he was residing, fall into Franco's hands! The sick man was packed off to jail without further ado, and has been there ever since. His wife, who knew even less than her husband about Spanish politics, was thrown into a dungeon so that her husband's plight might not reach the ears of the American Consular agent in the city.

Both were held for months without the slightest hope of escape — without trial — without even a charge filed against them. Evidently, they were not allowed to write.

Just how the prisoner conceived the idea of the Christmas card which is reproduced here, and how long it took him to make it will not be known until he is once more free. However, on this occasion his jailers allowed him to send Christmas greetings to his family in the United States.

The anxious relatives in New York received the card with surprise. It had not been his habit to write meaningless verse on decorated Christmas cards; he knew a letter would be much more welcome to them.

They saw the words "Merry Christmas" and "Happy New Year" written in a shaking hand — in fear and trembling. They saw that the doves of peace carrying the "Merry Christmas" banner were also carrying a letter. Somewhere a message must be contained in the red and black scribblings on the card. It became evident to them that the red scribblings were the key to this message. The doves turned out to be not doves, but carrier pigeons. Under the very wings of the pigeons the first message was easily deciphered.

On the lower wing of the right hand pigeon the scribblings that form the feathers spell: A U N. The left pigeon's lower wing very clearly has the word: F A C I O. The first letter F forms the lower part of the body. These two words: "Aun Facio" mean: Fascism is still here. How did he know in his prison cell that the fascist attack on Spain had become a war of the nations and was not a forgotten conflict on the Iberian Peninsula?

In the foliage on the left of the poem, several words can be deciphered among the twigs and flowers. In the third blossoming flower, counting from upper left to right, three letters are very

182

plain: I, U and D. This stands for the Spanish word Ayuda, meaning Help. Right below that flower appears the word Ella, meaning: Her. "Help Her": he is referring to his wife. The word HELL appears very plainly under the word Ella, after that the puzzle becomes more difficult and one can only guess.

But this information sufficed for the relatives in New York. They knew now where man and wife were to be found. The State Department in Washington, D.C. was informed, and a consular representative saw both the imprisoned man and his wife. Their American citizenship was acknowledged. Many letters went back and forth between relatives and the State Department in Washington, D. C.

Yet, as this book goes to press, both of these people, who did nothing to incur the wrath of rebel authorities, are still forgotten in the old dungeons of a Spanish jail.

TERESA AZNAR is a young woman of twenty-six who was born in a village near Saragossa. When still a child her parents brought her to the United States where she received her schooling. She was married in 1929. With her little son, Pedro, who was five years old when this letter was written, she went to visit her mother and father who had returned to Spain to live.

After some three months in Spain the military rebellion caught her in its net. It took several months before she was able to escape to France. This letter was written to a sister-in-law in New York City immediately upon her arrival in Paris. The most interesting part of this letter is contained in the postscript.

Unamuno, one of Spain's foremost philosophers, was one of the few intellectuals who sided with the insurgent generals. He had long been wavering on the side of fascism. Reports of his death reached the outside world in January 1937. This is the first time that the mysterious grapevine telegraph brings the news that perhaps Unamuno did not die in bed, that perhaps the very fascism of which he had been a champion in theory had killed him because it had revolted him in practice.

From Spanish Trenches

Paris, January 3, 1937

Dear Pilar:

The relief of escaping from the clutches of the fascists is spoiled by the sad news which I got from you. You cannot imagine what it means to live in the fascist inferno for all these months, to live under constant tension, fearful of the smallest noise and any knock on the door; saying to each other: "They have come for us". In Aranda de Duero it was something awful, they took our orchard and house away from us and put Carmen into jail for four days. After making her pay ten thousand pesetas they let her go. They constantly, at all times, came to search the house. Whenever a plane flew over the village, they said that it was our fault. In other words, it was plain madness. Those men with their guns hounded us and watched our house day and night. Finally we got to Burgos on the first of October. Here the repression was less severe at first, but when they saw that they couldn't take Madrid, they started again in the most frightful way. Every day they take from eighteen to twenty people from the jail and shoot them without trial and leave the bodies lying on the road. It isn't only workers they shoot but any republicans — doctors, teachers, or professors — they can lay their hands on. You can't imagine anything worse happening. Eighty percent of the teachers were thrown out of work, fifty percent of them were shot. In Salamanca, they killed two professors of the Normal School that way, one school inspector, and I don't know how many teachers. All you have to do is to say that you are a teacher and they arrest you. I wanted to find a doctor for little Pedro but I found that all the good ones were in jail with fines of forty and thirty thousand duros. [One duro equals five pesetas.]

From that point of view they have done a good job because they have thrown all the intelligent and neutral people out of their camp by their methods with the result that they have turned against them completely. In almost every family somebody has been killed. But what horrible methods. First they pull their arms and legs out of joint, then they beat them up, make them drunk with cognac, and finally kill them . . . Dreadful! Dreadful! In Valladolid and in Palencia it has been even worse. One of our friends, coming from Palencia, told us that he saw the bodies of seventeen women in the morgue there, and that three of them had been pregnant.

In many instances, they had killed both man and wife, he told me, and especially teachers. Oh, how can I tell you, in Begar they left forty children fatherless in one night. In one whole street there were only two couples left alive. I heard that the Protestant preacher in Salamanca has been killed, Freemasons were treated likewise. Julia was arrested again in Burgos, and only because she belonged to the Civil Liberties Union. They kept her in jail for ten days, finally they let her out, but she has to report to the police station every week and cannot leave the city. If they win, which I don't believe they will, nothing will happen to her, but if they lose . . . I don't want to think about it.

This kind of savagery behind the front is responsible for the hostile atmosphere that exists and it is also the cause for the low morale amongst the soldiers, for almost every soldier has had some member of his family murdered. Besides, they feed them very badly and they haven't enough clothes.

I am of the opinion that unless Germany helps them openly and with plenty of men they cannot triumph. There are very few Moors left, most of them have been annihilated and until now the Germans that I have seen in Burgos do not inspire fear — their morale is very low and they give the impression that they do not know what they are fighting for. They are so weak that it will be a pity if we do not defeat them. I am very sorry that I can't be with you right now. Kisses to all of you,

TERESA

P.S. Our friend from Palencia told me before I left that Unamuno is infuriated against them now and ascribes the biggest atrocities to them. He saw him only a few days before he spoke to me. They are having him watched very carefully and the police have orders to shoot him if he tries to get into a car.

UNDERSTANDING SPAIN

No matter what I am going to say I will be denounced as a violent Red, a member of the sinister forces that plot to destroy civilization. A government elected by the people may be attacked today with impunity and anyone who rises in its defense may be denounced as an agitator. I do not desire in the least to be an agitator, nor have I ever brought myself to join any political organization, right or left.

Yesterday something happened that gave me some hope. There were a number of us gathered together, talking about the situation in Spain. Someone said, "The *New York Times* is the newspaper which is most favorable to the Loyalist cause." Everyone looked up in surprise. Certainly the editorial policy was rather far removed from actual sympathy with the Spanish government and its aims. There was a momentary buzz in the room. "Wait a minute," he said, "let me explain. The reason I say the *New York Times* is most favorable to the Loyalists is because the *Times* prints *more news* than any other newspaper in this country. The more news that is printed about Spain, the more favorable the news appears for the government; it is only by omitting news — as the yellow press does — that you can keep the people in the dark."

No matter how much news is printed about the rebels, they will hardly be endeared to the general public. They somehow never seem to do anything magnanimous, unless you consider the bombing of unprotected cities and machine gunning fleeing civilians acts of kindness. And I am afraid the public tires of reading day in and day out the dispatch that a particular offensive will be completed as soon as fog and rain clear up. Why mention fog and ignore that determined army that would rather die on the battlefield than be robbed of freedom? No, the more news, the more favorable it must be to the government elected by the people.

But I would rather show you the kaleidoscope of Spain's history, so often jumbled and confused, but always brilliant in the sun which beats down on the mountain tops that divide Spain into an agglomeration of nations.

Understanding Spain

THE IBERIAN PENINSULA IN THE MIDDLE AGES

Here we do not deal with merely two countries: Spain and Portugal. Spain is divided by vast mountain ranges into a number of small sections in which early peoples lived with but very little knowledge of their neighbors. The high crests were hard to scale, the valleys were fertile, and thus these natural barriers were guarantees of peace for cultivation of the soil. Through the centuries these isolated groups developed their own language, their own culture and habits, and they have never quite lost them. Perhaps this, in addition to contributing political and economic causes such as lingering peasant and artisan modes of production, is a reason for individualist traits in the Spaniard. It explains the comparatively large number of anarchists in Spain as against other countries. Specific historic conditions retarded the large-scale industrialization of Spain. This industrialization would have eliminated the semifeudal economy which existed until the outbreak of the fascist counter revolution. Yet today we know from authoritative sources that most of these anarchists support the Popular Front government which they helped to elect.

Yet, today, we still have those Estramadurians, those Castilians and Murcians, Aragonese, Basques, and Catalonians. They are different in nature and custom and language. In the past their greatest handicap was their contempt of their neighbors' fate so long as they themselves were left alone in their valley.

In the Eighth Century the Moors began their conquest of the Peninsula. They were materially aided by the individualism of its inhabitants. Since the Spaniards refused to come to the aid of those who lived on the other side of the mountain, it was possible for the Moors to subjugate one small group after the other. Individually, the Spaniards continued to fight, killing their invaders whenever they could under cover of darkness, coming forth from their mountain recesses in sudden, swift, deadly attacks. It would take many centuries before they would learn that they could be invincible if they united in common purpose. Indeed, it took them eight centuries to drive the Moors back across the Straits of Gibraltar, and they will probably never rid themselves of the imprint which the invaders from another continent left on their mode of life.

From Spanish Trenches

But it is ridiculous to consider the horrible cruelty which is practiced *as a policy* by Franco and his fascist associates as a characteristic of "Spanish" Fascism. Such a technique is the universal policy of International Fascism. If there are incidents of cruelty on the Loyalist side, we know they are acts of individual hate, for it has been the policy of the government since the beginning of the outbreak to fight all acts of individual terrorism.

However, the consequences of the long struggle against Mohammedanism can be seen in the extremes of the Inquisition. The popular support which this received was due to the heritage of hate against Mohammedan conquerors, but the lords of the Church, acting in league with the barons of the land, extended the purposes of the Inquisition to include the atrocious persecution of the Jews, who were becoming too powerful as a merchant class. The masters of the feudal castles did not desire the power of finance to pass into the hands of individuals other than themselves.

During the latter part of the Fifteenth Century most of Spain's provinces were united under the rule of King Ferdinand of Aragon and Queen Isabella of Castile, man and wife. Only Viscaya and Catalonia continued their fierce struggle for independence which lasted throughout the next four centuries. Fighting and the riotous, luxurious living of the nobles bled the people dry. The Spanish Kingdom was forever threatened with destruction.

A strange whim possessed Isabella, when she took gold out of her almost empty coffers to finance the voyage of Columbus to India. But her whim resulted in the discovery of incredible riches. Columbus claimed the Americas for Isabella. Isabella sent her ships with orders to return them loaded with gold. Spain's nobility blossomed under this golden shower, its vassals were momentarily forgotten; they went back to the fields and to their trades to produce all the luxuries that the new wealth demanded for its owners. A stronger kingdom was built on stolen gold. Little did the Spanish rulers worry if in far away America the Indians bled to death amid the ruins of their ancient and proud civilization.

Catalonia alone continued its normal development and fought off all aggression from without. Since it was not drunk with the gold that could be had for the spilling of blood, it had to develop its own resources. While the rest of Spain resisted the introduction of bourgeois industry, Catalonia kept up with the progress of other European nations. Industry flourished and Catalonian ships plied the seven seas. While the Spaniard was the miserable slave of the landowner — the grandee — the Catalonian was free and proud. But in their industrious endeavor the Catalonians forgot that they were but a small nation, that their neighbor, who looked upon this choice morsel with envy, was a most powerful antagonist. Early in the Eighteenth Century, the kingdom of Spain subjected Catalonia to its rule. But it could never subject the Catalonians. They never forgot that they were a free people; they could not be forced to speak the hated Castilian or to acknowledge the Bourbon flag of those who ruled Spain.

Nor did the Spanish kings have to fear rebellion in Catalonia alone. All over the kingdom there was constant insurrection, a struggle against the unbearable oppression under which all the Spanish people lived. That struggle still rages today. There has never been a period of peace and acceptance for the masses of Spain. Today they merely continue to fight a battle which started many centuries ago. Perhaps that is why the revolutionary spirit is so much more developed today in Spain than elsewhere. Perhaps that is why the Spaniard would rather die than to return to the life which he has led ever since the days that the Moors first came to his mountains and valleys.

Later, in the first years of the Nineteenth Century, it was Napoleon who coveted the Iberian Peninsula for a French province. But little though they cared for their own rulers, even less did these people cherish the idea of another foreign invasion. They drove Napoleon's well-armed soldiers from the mountain crests with pitchforks and stones and for the first time they discovered that in unity they could defeat the strongest enemy. It had taken them many centuries to learn this lesson, but at last they knew, nor would they soon forget it.

THE CONSTITUTION

The Spanish people began fighting for a Constitution several centuries ago. The ease with which the various uprisings were quelled could not deter a people driven to desperation. There was no question of agitators responsible for the uprisings. It was the inability of

189

the poor to make even the barest living that drove them to their desperate and seemingly hopeless actions.

The army was built on the knowledge of the hate which existed between the inhabitants of the various provinces in Spain. Murcians hated Catalonians, so that they were unable to see their common cause in the blindness of their rage. The same was true of the other provinces. The senoritos — sons of the Spanish grandees — made use of this knowledge in the placement of their troops.

The unity of action which had caused the defeat of Napoleon's army in 1808, brought the crying need for unity to the Spanish people. In the midst of the invasion by the French, a constitution was decreed for the first time and an assembly set up. This assembly was called the *Cortes,* a name it still bears today. Once again, however, the individualism of the Spaniard defeated his plans for a democratic government. Once the cornerstone of the Republic was laid, they considered that henceforth the *Cortes* must take care of itself, as well as of the rest of the people in Spain. This illusion cost the Spanish people a democratic setback of more than a hundred years, and it is probably partly responsible for the 1936 monarchist-fascist rebellion.

Since the grandees of Spain were gradually losing their American pot of gold, they once more began seriously to hunt for better possibilities to exploit at home. They decided that ruthless suppression alone would guarantee them the luxuries and the power to which they had grown accustomed. Their plan of action was divided into two parts. The first one was the concentration of arms into one army, carefully officered by the sons of the nobility — the senoritos — and their immediate loyal supporters. In order to be absolutely sure that no treason could come from within the ranks of the soldiers there was a disproportionately large number of commissioned officers, whose tasks were very simple, because of the small group of men under their command.

The second part of this campaign for power required the assistance of the Church. Education for the common people came solely through the schools established by the clergy. Too much education would tend to develop too great a consciousness of the errors on which their society was based. This second part of the campaign was achieved by the peaceful penetration of the Church. It became a custom that, of the sons of a grandee, at least one would lay aside a career of arms to serve God. In the folds of a Bishop's robe he could take excellent care of his father's and brothers' interests; in return for his services the State paid him a truly kingly remuneration. The Church prospered. The toilers paid the taxes which supplied the salaries of clergy and officers, and again they would pay for the masses and the services which were held in the towering houses of God, built with the money of those who lived in their hovels on the bread and sour wine, the rancid olive oil and the corn that was left them for sustenance. Religion was saved and education for the people was primitive beyond words.

The Church of Spain could indeed praise the Lord for his kindness. Together with the army it was in complete control of every living soul in Spain, and it could pride itself on owning one-third of the national wealth. Some might criticize it for its rapaciousness. But was it not right to give the people a sample of heaven on earth, at least? If they could not taste it, one could let them see what the kingdom of heaven — to which all aspired — looked like.

In Spain the people struggled on, their ingratitude to their benefactors became ever more pronounced, their materialistic viewpoint became ever more alarming to the constantly weakening parade of Spanish kings. Attempts to establish a Republic were frequent. The Republicans were defeated in 1871, but at last triumphed in 1873, when King Amadeo retreated before the wrath of the people in very much the same way as Alphonso did in 1931.

Again the people were not ready to assume the responsibility of self government. Two years later the Republic collapsed when Alphonso XII ascended the Spanish throne. He reigned for ten years. Six months after the King's death, Alphonso XIII became the new king of Spain. Little did it matter whether a baby in his carriage, a boy in his teens or a grown Alphonso sat on the throne. The heavy hand of the dictatorship which ruled Spain did not relinquish its hold, nor did the voice of the people ever desist from denouncing the monarchy.

On April 14th, 1931, the day of the elections, the threatening rumble from the people of Spain in their demand for liberal legislation became too much for the king. That same night a fast automobile, with blinds drawn, transported him from Madrid across the

From Spanish Trenches

French border. Alphonso XIII had fled. He did not abdicate, he ran for his life and promised the Spanish people in a proclamation issued a few days later, that they would hear from him. There is no doubt that he has kept his promise.

On April 15th a provisional cabinet was set up, containing a large number of the progressive elements. Yet the Right was also represented. The desire for fair play always seems to influence democratic governments and allows participation by the worst enemies of Democracy.

A fiesta spirit had taken hold of Spain. There could be no doubt about the sentiments of the population, of their relief at being freed from the oppression of an authoritarian government. Yet today reactionaries all over the world dare to insinuate that a large part of the Spanish people desires to be ruled by just such a government of force.

Would the people be so capricious as to wish once more for a form of government that they had fought ferociously for many centuries? Significant is the fact that in the celebration all the old enmity was forgotten. No reprisals of any sort were taken by the people against their oppressors; they were satisfied to look to the future and to hope that from this moment on they could start to live.

Three months after the downfall of the Monarchy, the new *Cortes* was elected. For each fifty thousand of the total population, one deputy was elected. This method allowed for four hundred and seventy-three deputies, the same number which still forms the *Cortes* today. Before the advent of the Republic, the villages had been allowed a larger number of representatives in proportion to their population than the industrial centers. This, of course, was changed now, so that every citizen of Spain got the same right of representation. Of the four hundred and seventy-three seats in the *Cortes*, sixty went to the reactionary Right. I mention this merely as a reflection of the sentiment in favor of a democratic state. Much time and care was given to the creation of a constitution which would give equal rights to all the inhabitants of the country.

The drafted constitution was finally ratified and adopted by the *Cortes* in December of that same year. It embodied the principles of all democratic constitutions. Church and State were to be separated, freedom of religious worship was guaranteed, as well as freedom of speech and press. One of the new laws abolished child labor, and certain forms of social security were taken into consideration. The president of the Republic was to be elected for a period of six years, by the *Cortes* and by a group of electors equal in number to the *Cortes*.

No radical measures of any kind were adopted in the Constitution. In proof of this it need only be pointed out that no agrarian reforms were contemplated, much less any regulations to curb capitalism.

The era of the Republic had begun. It should only be necessary now to plant firmly the new freedom and to enjoy its fruits.

THE REACTION PLOTS

The grandees of Spain were left in possession of their lands and of the power which they exercised over their employees in industry. They sat in their ancient manor halls and mused. For them the Republic boded no good. Eventually their power would wane as the voice of the common people became articulate and more powerful. Under Marcelino Domingo and Dr. Fernandos de Los Rios a multitude of schools and libraries were being built all over the country. Certainly an educated peasant or factory worker would be most unwilling to continue to subsist on a daily wage of twenty cents and often less. Furthermore, these public schools were going to weaken the ties between the people and the Church which, even with Heaven in the perspective, was most unwilling to part with its earthly treasures. Together grandees and bishops decried public school education and the reading of books as an invention of Satan, and a call was issued to the faithful to beware of the innovations brought about by the constitution. The same Spain was speaking which had burned a man at the stake because he had dared to assert that the earth was round and not flat. Again the religion of the people was used to invoke a campaign of hatred against everything new.

Thus a united front of all the reactionary forces of the Iberian peninsula — grandee-landowners, monarchists, capitalists and above all the Church — was formed, and the Church's power to evoke fear and submission was exerted to its fullest by these groups to organize a defeat of the Republic and the powerful trade union movement. The voice of reaction became stronger, and with it grew the hopes of getting the people to destroy the Republic with the same hands that had fought so bitterly for many centuries to establish it. In the name of God, men and women of voting age were asked to endorse the exploitation of the landlords and of the industrial barons. There was to be no middle road to heaven for those who supported the Republic.

During the time that this campaign continued, the trade unions were being built into constantly stronger organizations. They would have been the safeguard of the Republic had they been allowed to survive long enough. From 1931 to the time of the elections in 1933, wages rose steadily along with the building of educational projects, and it looked as though at last the people of Spain would raise themselves to the material level of their European neighbors. However, the farm population did not keep pace with the industrial centers. Strangely enough, the señoritos were allowed to remain in command of the army. They had merely been requested to swear an oath of allegiance to the Republic, which most of them promptly did, including Francisco Franco, Emilio Mola and Queipo de Llano. The few arch-enemies of the Republic who were exiled or who fled from the country went to Italy and later to Germany for guidance in the new fascist demagogy which spoke words of socialism while it ruthlessly suppressed all the basic democratic rights of the people. This form of government was approved by all those who hated the Republic. The voice of the Church — that same Church which owned one-third of the nation's wealth — became heard in Gil Robles' *Accion Catolica*, which he organized early in 1932 and which later became a part of the CEDA (Spanish Confederation of Autonomous Right Parties). The representatives of the nobles and of the Church were preparing for action.

DEMOCRACY THROTTLED

The confidence of the Republicans in their government was so complete that no one was prepared for the outcome of the 1933 Fall elections. That is, no one except the Right parties that had engineered it. Their contempt of the masses was so great that they were not even surprised at their victory.

Lerroux became Prime Minister. His reputation as a Republican was far from praiseworthy. One's confidence in this government

194

would diminish with the knowledge that Gil Robles exerted considerable pressure on the cabinet. The enemies of the Republic, who had fled with the fall of the Monarchy, were allowed to return to Spain. Government subsidies to the already fabulously rich Church were reinstated. Efforts were being made once more to merge completely the State of Catalonia with the Spanish State, although it had but a short while ago achieved autonomy. This move was unsuccessful, for the strong trade-union and peasant movements of industrialized Catalonia could not as easily be led around by the nose. Catalonia continued to do the work that had been halted in the rest of the Republic, and agrarian reforms and better conditions for industrial workers were advocated and put into effect by its advanced political parties.

In Madrid, the political cauldron boiled over. The Lerroux Cabinet collapsed. Nor did the new Semper cabinet have much opportunity to prosper under the ever-increasing pressure from Gil Robles, who came backed by the money of the rich landlords and the infinite resources of the Church.

The threat of a fascist dictatorship along Italo-German lines became more menacing from day to day. Desperately the people of Spain saw only one way out: a Farmer-Labor government must be established before fascism could abolish all the rights which they had won with the Republic. Gil Robles knew and openly admitted that his machinations in the government were responsible for the uprisings which mushroomed all over the country. He willingly encouraged these uprisings of 1934, which cost thousands of human lives, and were most severe in Asturia. Rather than to allow the people time in which to form a popular government, Robles permitted dissension to bring on a civil strife which would form an excuse for the establishment of the fascist dictatorship which the Rightists coveted.

Although the blood-bath in which the 1934 uprisings resulted was one of the most terrific mass murders in history, Robles did not realize his hopes of a dictatorship. He had not reckoned with the enraged determination for freedom, intensified by centuries of struggle. The people of Spain had reawakened—they had realized that this was no time for sleep, that only continuous vigilance could defeat the purpose of the assembled enemies of the people. From a soil irrigated with blood rose the Popular Front of Spain.

February 1936 Elections

The victory of the Front Populaire in July 1935 in France became an inspiration to the Spanish masses. They decided that they must act likewise. Parties which had refused to meet or to cooperate under any circumstances forgot their individual grievances for a common stand against the repression which had followed the puppet government of Gil Robles and his CEDA. It now became a question for the Republicans to compromise rather than to lose every last vestige of the freedom for which they had fought so long. The thirty thousand political prisoners, thrown into jail by the party in power, had among them members from all the political parties represented in the Frente Popular. They were a constant, grim reminder that action must be taken and must be taken soon.

This popular front was far from being radical in its demands. Because of the reluctance of the absentee landlord to rent his land at a low price, the burden of the farmer had to be eased. The courts were badly in need of reform before they could uphold the guarantees which had been given the people by the Constitution. A public works program was also needed in order to reduce the number of unemployed all over the country. None of these measures will sound very strange or radical to Americans who endorsed and participated in the Roosevelt landslide of 1936.

These were the measures which brought the Spanish people to vote in favor of the Popular Front on February 16, 1936. The moment had come for reaction to realize its defeat and to retire gracefully. But all reports seem to indicate that they took just the opposite road. From the very moment they were beaten at the polls, they plotted and schemed to get the government into their hands once more, this time by force of arms.

Now let us have a look at the different parties which formed the Popular Front. The Socialists, who in Spain were a mild body of Social Democrats, similar in many ways to the progressive wing of our Democratic party, gained 89 seats in the new *Cortes*. The Left Republicans — we would compare them to our Centerist 1936 Democrats — elected 83 representatives; the more conservative

Republicans 34. The Catalonian Republicans got 22 seats. Against this large number of more or less conservative bodies the Communists of Spain obtained only 14 seats and were not represented at all in the first cabinet which was formed. With other progressive parties the Popular Front elected 260 deputies to the *Cortes.* Altogether, the Rightists polled enough votes to elect 147 representatives, a little more than half the number won by the Popular Front. Various Center parties, whose sympathies are probably more or less evenly divided, got the remaining 66 seats.

Yet it is an accepted fact that the minority groups of Rightists began to prepare to regain the power which they had lost at the polls in February 1936 as soon as they realized just how badly they had been beaten. They prepared their plans very carefully. They knew that the army could be depended on to do their bidding, but that it would be essential to strike in all Spanish cities simultaneously to seize the governments of all the important cities. Only in that way would it become impossible for the population to collect its unorganized forces. When they struck on July 18, 1936, their action seemed to be premature. Why did they strike so soon? There was probably more than one reason. Perhaps their plot was about to be exposed. It would have been fatal to attack a government which was prepared, and it would have been but a matter of hours for the Popular Front to build an adequate defense.

The pretext used by the fascists for the uprising was certainly very thin. Calvo Sotelo, ex-finance minister, outspoken enemy of the people, had been found dead in a Madrid graveyard. Was it the action of fascist provocateurs or was he killed by the infuriated shock-police of Madrid, in retaliation for the murder of their beloved leader, José De Costillo? We will probably never know. The cause of his death matters little. The fact that counts is that men who had sworn allegiance to the government but a few months ago now rose up to annihilate this same government. On July 14th, Gil Robles yelled at the body of the *Cortes:* "Our wrath will fall upon the parties which support you in the Popular Front coalition and will spatter the whole regime with mud, with misery and with blood." On his way to Portugal he found time to stop long enough in Paris to inform interviewers that he had no hand in the military rebellion.

From Spanish Trenches

Franco and the other generals were much more frank. Before the end of July all of them admitted that their program was to institute a military dictatorship, to suppress all trade unions, to abolish the *Cortes* as well as the cabinet, and to cancel any kind of land division heretofore decreed: "Because the peasants are too poor to cultivate poor land . . . Perhaps twenty-five years from now." (Franco in an interview immediately after the uprising.) Viscaya and Catalonia would lose the partial independence which had been granted them by the Republic. In other words, this program would take Spain back directly to the period before the establishment of the Republic in 1931. Small wonder then that the Spanish people stormed machine gun nests with their bare hands, and defeated their enemy with practically no weapons during that first month following the insurrection. If this had merely been a civil war . . .

But already on the day before July 18th there were authentic reports that Italian planes were on their way to assist Franco in his attempt to dominate Spain. Within a few days Germany was known to be sending equipment by the shipload. Shipments of war machinery and men followed each other in an ever-increasing stream. Herein lies the horror of the war in Spain. It has become the testing ground of fascist war machinery. Factory owners send representatives to correct weaknesses in their equipment, which hitherto had not been tried out on living subjects and on real objects like the villages and cities of Spain. And that is not the only benefit which fascist governments derive from their assistance. Franco is willing to promise almost anything to his fascist friends; he has become the hired agent of Germany and Italy. If he is victorious, Spain will no longer belong to the Spanish people; it will be another colony added to the power-thirsty fascist empire.

I do not desire to delve into the massacre that has taken place in Spain this last year. Nor need I recall Franco's words on August 16, 1936: "I will not bombard Madrid . . . there are innocent people there." I am not going to resurrect the horrors of Badajoz, of Guernica, Málaga, Almeria and countless other places that may not be found on your map, but that were inhabited by live human beings, who wanted to live, who had little children, babies in cribs . . . Five hundred thousand of them are no longer alive today. They keep passing before my eyes — one out of every fifty inhabitants of the entire Spanish Republic.

And all this time a voice hammers at my ears. It is the voice of Louis Delaprée, French newspaperman:

"The strongest sentiment that I experienced today was neither fear, nor anger, nor compassion:

"It was shame.

"I am ashamed of being a human being when humanity shows itself capable of such massacres of innocents."

Yes, Louis Delaprée, we should be ashamed of being part of a society which allows this to go on. We should be ashamed that we are able to eat and drink and sleep and walk about while a whole race is being exterminated by the Fascist International.

BLUE SEAL BOOKS

1. BABIES WITHOUT TAILS, *by Walter Duranty*
2. ALL'S FAIR, *by Richard Wormser*
3. MURDER STRIKES THREE, *by David MacDuff*
4. OLD HELL, *by Emmett Gowen*
5. RED FEATHER, *by Marjorie Fischer* (Juvenile)
6. MEALS ON WHEELS, *by Lou Willson and Olive Hoover* (Cook Book)

GOLD SEAL BOOKS

1. THE UNITED STATES: A GRAPHIC HISTORY, *by Louis M. Hacker, Rudolf Modley and George R. Taylor*
2. FROM SPANISH TRENCHES, *compiled by Marcel Acier*
3. KALTENBORN EDITS THE NEWS, *by H. V. Kaltenborn*
4. THE LABOR SPY RACKET, *by Leo Huberman*
5. MEN WHO LEAD LABOR, *by Bruce Minton and John Stuart*

RED SEAL BOOKS

1. TRAVELS IN THE CONGO, *by André Gide*
2. TWELVE AGAINST THE GODS, *by William Bolitho*
3. SUSPICIOUS CHARACTERS, *by Dorothy L. Sayers*
4. THE LEAVENWORTH CASE, *by Anna Katharine Green*
5. THEY SHALL INHERIT THE EARTH, *by Morley Callaghan*
6. THE DARING YOUNG MAN ON THE FLYING TRAPEZE, *by William Saroyan*
7. THE HONORABLE PICNIC, *by Thomas Raucat*
8. MR. WESTON'S GOOD WINE, *by T. F. Powys*
9. A PASSAGE TO INDIA, *by E. M. Forster*
10. BLOOD OF THE CONQUERORS, *by Harvey Fergusson*

 # MODERN AGE BOOKS

IT would cost several thousand dollars to publish a single book. When the cost is spread over two or three thousand books, as is usually the case, the cost per book is reduced, but still remains high enough to put it beyond the reach of the average reader.

To overcome this difficulty, Modern Age Books are printed in editions of fifty to a hundred thousand copies, which so reduces the cost per book that it is possible to sell them at a price well adapted to the average pocketbook.

Modern Age Books are being published at regular intervals. They are full-length books, by the best modern authors. They cover the entire field of current literature from popular fiction to serious studies of political, social, and economic problems. In addition to new books, Modern Age is re-issuing a series of unabridged editions of the literary treasures of the present and the past.

For the purpose of convenient identification, all Modern Age Books are issued in three classifications: 1. Blue Seal Books; 2. Gold Seal Books; 3. Red Seal Books. All new books published for sale at 25¢ carry the Blue Seal label; all new books priced above 25¢ carry the Gold Seal label; all re-issues of standard literary works carry the Red Seal label.

All books published in these three classifications at these low prices are bound in sturdy paper covers. For those who wish to have Modern Age Books in a more durable form, a limited number of both Blue and Gold Seal titles are available, attractively bound in cloth.

10.50